FLY HIGH, FLY FAST, FLY FAR!

हर दिन, हर रात, हर पल!

FLIGHT PLAN

TO SUCCESS

SEAL THE WIN BEFORE YOU BEGIN
AND ACCOMPLISH ANY GOAL

JT DeBOLT

Flight Plan to Success:
Seal The Win Before You Begin And Accomplish Any Goal
by JT DeBolt

Disclaimer: This publication is designed to provide accurate and authori-
tative information regarding the subject matter. The author and /or publisher disclaim any and all liability, directly or indirectly, for advice and
information presented herein. The author and/or publisher do not assume
any responsibility for errors, omissions, or interpretation of the subject
matter herein.

ISBN 978-1-61206-000-2

Cover Design: Cari Campbell, Cari Campbell Design
Interior Layout: Shiloh Schroeder, Fusion Creative Works
Primary Editor: Mia DeBolt

For more information, or to purchase in bulk, contact: jt@jtdebolt.com
or visit www.FlightPlantoSuccess.com

Published by

AlohaPublishing.com

Second Printing
Printed in the United States of America

DEDICATION

This book is dedicated to my amazing wife, Mia. My best friend, my soul mate, my passionate partner--thank you for always believing in me. Thank you for pushing me to always grow and be my personal best. Thank you for your wisdom, your compassion and your laughter. Thank you for always seeing the beauty in life. Thank you for our amazing kids, Callie Jean and Maximus. Thank you for being my co-pilot and my navigator in the skies most people never dare to fly.

ACKNOWLEDGMENTS

I'm humbled and honored to be surrounded daily by High-Altitude people who are as committed to my mission as they are to their own. Their influence lives throughout the pages of this book and in nearly every facet of my life. As you are about to read, I'm truly blessed.

First, I want to thank my amazing and supportive family:

- To my beautiful and talented wife, Mia: Thank you for being my muse, my confidante, my voice of reason, and my biggest supporter. You are the one who saw the vision before anyone else, and encouraged my leap of faith from the "comforts" of Navy life to the uncharted waters of entrepreneurship. Your unwavering support makes it possible for me to do the work I love every single day. Your contributions to this book and to the direction of our business are profound; there is a part of you in every word I share, every step I take, and every person we touch with the message. I love you and am so grateful to have you as my soul mate.

- To my daughter, Callie, and son, Maximus. You are my inspiration and my joy. I see the future in your smiles and feel the power of the universe in your love. I love you and am humbled and grateful to be your daddy.

- To my dad, Robert DeBolt. Thank you for believing in me. Your support, love and encouragement have meant more to me than any other gifts you have given me in my life. I am grateful to be your son.

- To my mother, Doris Betsworth. Thank you for the encouragement and for reminding me to laugh. You share my love of flight and belief in dreams, and always fill my heart with happiness.

- To my brothers, Dan and Robby, and my sister, Kim Holloway. Thank you for being my cheering section, my stand-up comedians, and the best brothers and sister I could ever ask for. I love you!

- To Mia's wonderful parents, Tom and Mary Jo Smith. Thank you for your love, your generosity and for bringing so much joy and happiness to my life.

- To my aunt and uncle, Nancy and Peter Hartung. Your love, encouragement, and support have meant the world to me. Thank you for showing me what hard work, perseverance, and staying committed to your dream is all about. You are true champions.

- To my late step-mother, Pamela Hartung. You were a best friend and mentor and an example of courage, strength, and grace. Your influence lives on today in my thoughts, my words, and my vision. I love you and miss you.

- To my late grandfather Harold DeBolt. Thank you for being my hero and the example I strive to live up to. Thank you for your wisdom, unconditional and open love, and for the inspiration to fly.

I have been blessed to have had some truly phenomenal people lend their talents, time and resources to me in the writing of this book. Without them, this book would only be an idea:

- To Maryanna Young, my publisher, my mentor, and my friend. Thank you for your friendship, guidance, inspiration, wisdom, honesty, integrity, and generosity. You saw my vision and believed in me from the beginning. You give so freely and willingly always, and I am so grateful to call you a friend. Thank you for believing in me and this project. I could not have done it without you.

- To Cari Campbell, my graphic designer. Thank you for your capturing my vision so beautifully in your brilliant work. I am fortunate to have you on my team!

- To Shiloh Schroeder, my interior design specialist. Thank you for doing phenomenal work and your ability to respond on the fly to my last-minute changes. You personify mission accomplishment!

My life has been amazing, and I owe a great deal of gratitude to some people who have influenced and supported me for a very long time. Their talent and spirit have helped shaped who I am today:

- To Rene Kamstra, my amazing coach and dear friend. Thank you for a powerful foreword to this book! You believed in me even when I didn't. You taught me to see in the dark and trust when faith was the only way. You continue to bring the best of me to the surface and demonstrate how to strike a balance between creating a successful business and a life well-lived. I wouldn't be the coach or messenger I am today without your influence. With deep gratitude and love, I thank you, my friend.

- To Jim Ponder, my inspirational friend. Through your commitment and passion for all you do, you define the term *servant leader*. The excellence you bring to the business world is inspiring. Thank you for believing in the message and for flying on my wing.

- To Viliami Tuivai. You are a brother and a friend, a mentor and teammate in success. Through your inspiring example, I'm constantly reminded what it means to be a passionate leader, devoted husband, committed father, and a champion of life. I appreciate you, brother.

- To Lehman Hailey. One of my best friends in business and life, I am grateful for your wisdom and compassion, and your sense of humor when the pressure is on. Thank you for being there.

- To Jami Counter. Thank you for believing in me when nobody else did. Your hard work and dedication to my dream helped make it a reality.

- To Pat Dennis. Thank you for the gift of your friendship and the brotherly love I could always count on.

- To Capt. Paul Hennes, US Navy (ret). Thank you for being the finest naval officer I had the privilege to serve under and learn from. Your leadership and compassion inspire me to this day.

- To Capt. Steve Vahsen, USN. Thank you for your guidance and leadership, and for never giving up on me.

- To Capt. Leon Bacon, USN. Thank you for your compassion and support and for being instrumental in my flight career.

- To Dave Stech, Patrick Combs, Craig Zuber, and Cindy Sawyers. Thank you for the impact you've made in my life. I appreciate you all.

- To Lt. Col. Rob "Waldo" Waldman, USAF. Thanks for lending a wing when I needed it; your wisdom made a profound impact. You are a true wingman!

- To Gary Vaynerchuk. Thank you for waking me up.

- To Darren Hardy, thank you for your daily demonstration of excellence and vision. You have made a deep impact on my business and life through your work, and I am forever grateful to you.

- To the incredible men and women of the United States Armed Forces with whom I have had the privilege to serve. Thank you for your courage, your sacrifice and for being the best part of my career. Thank you for continuing to carry the torch.

- Despite my best efforts, I have undoubtedly forgotten some important people. I am, nonetheless, grateful to you and everything you have done for me. My life would not be as blessed without you. You know who you are...

GRATITUDE

The book you are holding in your hands contains more than the personal story of a kid with a dream who defied the odds and accomplished a childhood dream, it is the byproduct of the work I do with some remarkable human beings.

You are about to access real-world strategies, tested over time and put into action every day by amazing men and women all over the world. You are about to benefit from more than just my personal experience, but the experience of the High-Altitude People I have the privilege to call my clients.

These amazing people are much like you. They are entrepreneurs, athletes, authors, musicians, moms and dads, students, and teachers. They are visionaries: the dreamers that became doers by getting busy on the work required to make their dreams their reality. They have raised the bar in their lives, their businesses, their relationships, and their communities, and in so doing, have raised the collective level of excellence throughout the world. And they've had a huge influence on the information you are about to experience in this book through their own contributions, feedback, suggestions, and results.

To my clients, I say thank you. You have been instrumental in taking these strategies and processes to the next altitude with your focus, commitment, persistence, and passion. I am inspired by your faith in yourselves and your dreams, and your commitment to the message of Flight Plan To Success™.

There is a part of each of you in this book, and for that, I am honored, humbled, and eternally grateful. I appreciate you.

~JT

CONTENTS

FOREWORD

Being a top Executive Coach over the past 28 years has allowed me to work with thousands of people in over 27 countries. I've worked with Anthony Robbins and Chet Holmes organizations, as well as the Chairman of my own business. My experience has taught me to hear excellence when I encounter it.

I've worked with a wide range of people: some performing at the top of their game and some struggling to get back on track. No matter the situation I've been able to meet and work with outstanding people from all walks of life. I have been blessed to work with such people through my years in this wonderful calling and am grateful for the encounters that have allowed me to become part of their lives, whether it was an introduction, live event, or even an unplanned connection through the remarkable synergy that is life.

My first encounter with JT DeBolt was in 2011 while we were attending an exclusive event. Attendees included titans of the personal development and business growth industry. And here was JT, a man who had gone from combat-decorated Naval Aviator to start-up entrepreneur in the midst of one of the worst economic times since the Great Depression. From our initial encounter I knew there was something special about him. After a few minutes of conversation we both knew we'd be working together.

Despite the state of the nation's economy JT had a dream to share his powerful message with the world; he was the epitome of the entrepreneurial spirit. Here was a man not willing to allow other's views or even national status to keep him from sharing his message.

Having recently released his first edition of *Flight Plan To Success*, he was eager to change lives with his gift. JT sought my guidance to help him grow and get his message, his gift out there. Initially we worked in a coach-to-client capacity, but over time, we began to see how our combined talents could serve a greater audience. The result: the ability to deliver inspiring content as a team. To this day I consider JT more than a client and colleague, I consider him a friend.

This book is special for many reasons but most importantly because it is a beautiful blend of one man's personal journey from self-doubt and limiting beliefs to military leader to international speaker, executive success coach, and award-winning author. JT's coaching clients range from individuals to corporations and span the globe from the US to Australia, Canada, and Europe.

It has been my pleasure and honor to watch JT develop and refine his message and to see him grow and share that message. I feel this is the "most powerful message, that you never saw coming".

While yes, the big names in the industry of personal and professional development are easy to remember and even more exciting to cite, JT DeBolt is committed to helping people live their dreams through practical, challenging, and actionable lessons. This makes him unforgettable! And in short time, the world will begin to know his name. This is a man committed to helping people and organizations around the world accomplish their own missions.

As you turn each page you will begin to take the real world strategies on board in your own business and life, and you'll begin to see what I've seen for years emanating from JT DeBolt. These are more than messages, more than strategies.

Flight Plan To Success is the guide to defining one's purpose and building a simple yet powerful structure to get "unstuck" and finally accomplish the biggest goals you've held your entire life. This book is the real deal. It is a no-nonsense guide for the person serious about success, and when applied consistently, it has the power to transform your life.

I can confidently say this with no hype or fanfare because it isn't needed. The message in this book stands alone and speaks for itself.

Flight Plan To Success is the product of years of real-world applications and daily discipline. This daily discipline and applications are more than a result of JT's military career; they are also part of his own entrepreneurial success and that of his clients. JT's keen ability to relate to people on a personal level allows him to assess their challenges and bring a unique perspective to the table. This provides excellent options to help see a way to success that may have been "hidden" before. Now you too can benefit from that wisdom with JT DeBolt's *Flight Plan to Success.*

So settle in and buckle up for an amazing read. Take the knowledge herein to heart and put it into practice daily. Then you'll see what many have already discovered, as JT says, that "you have everything you need to accomplish anything you want."

Rene Kamstra
International Executive Coach and Entrepreneur

INTRODUCTION

The world needs more champions. The world needs more heroes. I'm not talking about the winners of trophies, nor men and women with the courage to run into a burning building to save a life or into a wall of gunfire to defend freedom.

I'm talking about ordinary people willing to step up and accomplish extraordinary things. People willing to boldly go for the dreams others have told them were ridiculous or impossible. People who know the status quo is unacceptable. For those who want to be excellent. For YOU.

Because for far too many, the status quo is a way of life.

The sleep walking hordes have made an agreement with themselves that they can live with whatever life gives them, no questions asked. When they fail, they simply shrug and say it wasn't meant to be.

If you are someone who is unwilling to live with what the status quo dictates is acceptable, if you have your eyes open and set on big dreams and big goals, and if you are tired of living a life that has not yet reached its full potential, then it's time to shift the momentum. It's time to find that significance you have been seeking and pursue it with certainty.

But this rally cry comes with a warning: the difference between dreamers and achievers is the *action* the achievers take consistently to realize their dreams. It requires risk. It requires courage. It requires pushing yourself beyond any point you've pushed past before. And achievers know that any significant endeavor requires a solid plan in order to succeed.

Unfortunately, few people actually plan their lives. Even fewer have a clear idea of what they want and set solid goals or take active steps toward achieving those goals. Instead, too many wake up every morning and go through the motions—until they look around to see a life of boredom, regret, and unhappiness. Too often, rather than reevaluating their lives, they simply turn to an escape to numb the pain and give away their power by blaming outside forces for their lot in life.

It's time to recalibrate this mindset.

I'm living proof that, with a flight plan—solid goals backed with *purpose* and steps to achieve that goal—you can accomplish any goal…

As a kid growing up in Boise, Idaho all I wanted to do was fly as a pilot in the US Navy's elite flight demonstration team—the Blue Angels. Some of the best fighter pilots in the world, the Blues display incredible feats of aviation excellence and conduct themselves with the utmost professionalism both in and out of the cockpit.

People constantly told me I wasn't cut out for it. After all, to be a Blue Angel meant becoming a Navy jet pilot. Becoming a Navy jet pilot meant being in the top of your flight school class. Being in the top of your flight school class meant getting into flight school, which required a commission as a naval officer, which required a college degree.

And truthfully, I was a horrible student who lacked focus.

"Diagnosed" with Attention Deficit Disorder (ADD), my grades were horrendous; people close to me—teachers, coaches, family, and friends—perhaps in an attempt to protect me from the disappointment of failure, told me I wasn't right for such a technical and academically demanding line of work. They suggested I keep my expectations "realistic" and settle for becoming an aircraft mechanic; that way I could still be around aviation and serve my country.

In an effort to show the world I meant business, I enlisted in the Navy right out of high school. The Navy sent me off to "A-School", the trade school where sailors learn their profession. In a twist of irony, the trade the Navy selected for me was aircraft mechanic! I took it in stride and saw it as an opportunity to connect with Naval Aviators and learn what it took to earn the Wings of Gold.

I worked hard, proved myself as an excellent mechanic, and applied six different times to become an officer, with the hopes of earning a slot to go to flight school. Superiors told me I was not right for the officer ranks. Mentors and direct supervisors told me I was dreaming if I ever thought I'd fly aircraft in the Navy.

But one person believed in me; my division officer, Jamie Counter. He backed me up and helped me put together package after package to the officer accession programs.

Every six months, I applied and reapplied to become an officer. Every application process was thorough and demanding. Every submission came with it the hope, the prayers, the anxiety...and the waiting.

And every application came back with the same response: "DENIED". All six times. Rejection after heart-wrenching rejection deepened my doubt as to whether or not I was, indeed, cut out for my dream. Were the doubters and naysayers right? Was I deluding myself by thinking I could make it as a Naval Aviator?

After four years of applying, reapplying, and working hard toward a dream that seemed would never come true, I had a tough decision to make. My enlistment contract was complete, and I had the choice of staying in the Navy and making a career as an aircraft mechanic or getting out and pursuing my dream a different way. Staying in meant career security, full benefits, regular paychecks, and routine promotions. Getting out offered only uncertainty.

I made the unpopular decision to get out, and then I went to work on my dream. I washed dishes and bussed tables in restaurants; I changed oil and rotated tires in automotive garages; I dug ditches and tore down old buildings for a construction firm. I was killing myself to make a living. But something deep down inside continued to burn—it was the thing that made my eyes turn skyward each time I heard the roar of jet noise overhead.

With the GI Bill—and some help from a few people who loved and believed in me—I did what few people would ever imagine: I went back to college. I excelled in math and science—something that amazed even me. I worked hard at a community college, got good grades, retook the SAT test, and gained acceptance to the University of Colorado in Boulder.

When I arrived in Boulder, I made an appointment with the Naval Reserve Officer Training Corps (NROTC) department. I told them I wanted to be an officer and a pilot. They advised me that I would have to earn a scholarship through academic and military performance, and that my chances were very low, as scholarships were few and far between.

With a generous gift of money from my grandfather—my personal hero who had flown B-17's in the European Theater during WWII—I had one last shot at my dream.

After my second semester at Colorado—after all the money had dried up and I was attending classes on borrowed time—I was one of four students awarded a full-ride scholarship. Three years later, I graduated with honors—the top graduate in my NROTC class—earning my degree, my commission as a naval officer, and an appointment to US Navy flight school.

On September 7, 2001—four days before the terrorist attacks of 9/11, I accomplished what most people in my life said I'd never accomplish—I was awarded my Wings of Gold and designated a Naval Aviator. My dreams had finally come true.

The strategies you are about to learn are the strategies that helped me realize my dream of becoming a Naval Aviator. The systems you'll learn are the same ones I used to plan surveillance and reconnaissance missions over Afghanistan, as well as ground operations in Iraq. And they have served me well as an entrepreneur, a father, and a passionate human being.

Now it's your turn to do the same.

It's time to stop listening to those who tell you your dreams are too big ... that your success was meant for others ... that you should lower your standards.

You are here on this earth for a reason. Everything has a purpose, especially you. You may or may not yet know what it is, but it is time to realize your purpose and go after your greatest masterpiece: your life mission.

"...because there is one great truth on this planet: whoever you are, or whatever it is that you do, when you really want something, it's because that desire originated in the soul of the universe. It's your mission on earth."
~Paulo Coelho, from *The Alchemist*

If you have big aspirations for your life, strap in, and get ready—the time has come for your dreams to take flight. And you, my friend, are the pilot of your destiny. If you are ready to take flight, the next step of your journey awaits. It's time for your Preflight Briefing!

~JT

CHAPTER 1

PREFLIGHT BRIEFING

The clouds hung low and heavy over the runway as we awaited clearance for takeoff. It had been a hectic afternoon, and we were eager to complete our mission and call it a day.

My co-pilot, a seasoned Naval Aviator, had carefully planned our flight and submitted a written description of our intentions—our flight plan—to the air traffic control (ATC) agency.

As we waited for the radio alert clearing us for takeoff, an ominous sight awaited us at the end of the runway: a solid wall of clouds obstructed the mountains ahead. Hovering a few hundred feet off the ground—just high enough to permit us to take off—the clouds hid the mountains completely. We would have to climb nearly 10,000 feet to reach clear skies; the mountains rose as high as 9,000 feet.

"Navy Seven-Two-Six, winds one-six-zero at five, you are cleared for takeoff." The air traffic controller cleared us for takeoff on a runway with a 5 knot headwind that blew just off the right side of the nose.

"Navy Seven-Two-Zero cleared for takeoff." My co-pilot responded.

We pushed up the throttles, the engines whined and the aircraft lurched forward. As we raced down the runway, I checked our airspeed and called, "Rotate," the command to pull back on the controls and fly the aircraft into the sky.

Within seconds, we were in the clouds, with zero reference to which way was up and which way was down. Due to the inertia of going from a dead stop to 150 miles per hour, my inner ear was lying to my brain, telling it we were in a left turn. The urge to turn right was strong, but one look at the gauges told me our wings were level and we were climbing nicely.

I checked the flight plan and verified it on the charts, or flight maps, to ensure we were not headed for disaster. It seemed like we were caught in the clouds for an hour as we climbed toward our assigned altitude of 11,000 feet.

My blood ran cold as I could envision a mountain racing toward us, giving us only seconds of terror prior to smashing us into bits. Suddenly, without warning, a bright flash of light illuminated the cockpit. We cleared the clouds, and could see the vast Pacific Ocean in the distance.

Careful planning, attention to detail, and staying the course allowed us to complete our mission—to fly a multimillion dollar airplane, into a cloud, directly at a towering mountain range, and come out safely and efficiently on the other end.

It can do the same for you.

Charting Your Flight Path To Success™

Piloting an airplane can be a high risk, dangerous activity. But despite the risk involved, people fly aircraft every day. They fly into the night, into foul weather... even into combat. And they do so not because they're crazy or brash, but because they're dedicated, courageous—and they're prepared.

Pilots always have a plan.

Your journey to success should be no different.

Success requires a concerted effort. Take a look at any tremendously successful person—Olympian, titan of business, famous musician or artist, anyone who has reached the pinnacle of achievement—and chances are they did not get to the top by happenstance or luck.

Success requires the courage first to dream, then to plan, then to execute that plan. There is risk associated with anything great. The risk of failure, the risk of losing money, position, and even one's life. The risks involved in achieving are part of the journey, and any champion of life who endeavors to do great things accepts and takes calculated risks.

The key is to understand the risk, and then prepare and plan around threats that may arise, so you can continue flying in the face of adversity to victory.

The Flight Plan

In aviation, a pilot uses a flight plan to chart their route of flight from their point of departure to their destination. In a nutshell, a flight plan consists of a clear mission—or a goal, backed by vision—and logical path to accomplish that mission. With careful planning of exact locations and precise timelines, pilots can fly in total darkness or stifling fog and land at their desired destination.

As a Naval Aviator, I used flight plans to execute everything from simple missions of flying from one airport to another, to complex missions of armed surveillance and reconnaissance over Afghanistan. Those flight plans gave my crew and me the ability to navigate dangerous skies and execute our missions with success.

Similarly, as a military liaison officer in Iraq, my team and I used a plan to execute incredibly complex tasks under arduous and dangerous circumstances to rebuild that country's oil infrastructure. Billions of dollars and precious human lives were on the line. A solid strategy was crucial to ensuring mission success.

In both situations the key to success was utilizing a strategy of combining the vision, planning, and execution of the plan.

The Importance Of A Flight Plan

No matter how great a pilot is (or thinks he is), he needs direction.

If you've ever driven with someone who's gotten lost and refused to ask for directions, you know how frustrating it can be. And if you've been the one to get lost, you know how awkward it can be to admit that you're lost—knowing your only way home is to ask for directions. C'mon, admit it—it's embarrassing!

Now imagine this: try flying a mission over Afghanistan, low enough to be shot down, with no real weapons for self-defense... and your future spouse is on board telling you where to go.

That was my life. Well, a chapter of my life. I met my wife, Mia, when I was a pilot in the Navy. Now when I say that, most people naturally assume this was the result of chance meeting in a bar or through a mutual acquaintance. In our case, the mutual acquaintance was the US Navy.

While she may have started off as a teammate and trusted friend, Mia was also my navigator. In fact, she went on to become a mission commander and tactical coordination officer responsible for oversight of all aspects of our missions with exception of safety of flight. Flying the aircraft was my job. To put it bluntly, I became her voice-activated auto-pilot.

But when flying over hostile territory, Mia adhered to procedures and was disciplined in sticking to our flight plan. Her diligence in monitoring our flight path saved our asses more than once, and enabled us to come home safely every time. She has a 100% success rate because she stuck to the flight plan.

You see, without a flight plan, pilots are more likely to get lost, run out of fuel, and crash. At the very least, they become limited in how far they can fly.

In military aviation, as well as any flight under Instrument Flight Rules (IFR), a concise flight plan is not only beneficial to the pilot, it's required by law.

Any professional pilot flying an important mission files a flight plan. Why should you be any different?

After all, the breakdown of any pursuit can often be linked to a lack of planning. And while flying by the seat of your pants is sometimes necessary, a solid plan for safely executing the mission is absolutely critical.

Therefore, if you're a professional when it comes to the pursuit of your dream—if your dream is important enough to pour 100% commitment into—then filing your own flight plan is not only a great idea, it's an absolute requirement.

Flying Through The Fog

Just as my co-pilot's flight plan enabled us to identify the barriers, in the form of mountains, and strategically chart our course safely between the peaks, your flight plan can enable you to navigate the barriers to your success.

Barriers to your success may include:

» The economy
» Experience
» Education
» Age
» Background
» Your past
» Spouse
» Health
» Time (or lack thereof)
» Financial situation
» Fear

As you set out toward fulfilling your dream, no doubt you'll encounter at least a couple on this list. When you do, you must plan to navigate your way around them. They may have stood in your way in the past, but that was then. This is now. The time for fear, self-doubt, and self-pity has passed. Now is the time to rise to the challenge of your greatest feat—to realize your true vision. Now is the time to let go of the past and drop the dead weight of excuses so you can climb into the air of high achievement.

It's time to win. It's time to fly toward your dreams.

How To Influence The Future

Have you ever noticed how some people respond differently to setbacks and stress than others? A financial blow, such as the loss of employment or an unexpected medical bill can be handled with grace and poise by one person, while a flat tire may send another into an emotional tailspin.

A good friend of mine experienced a failure of the oil system on one of his engines during a routine flight to Yuma, Arizona. He and his co-pilot went through the emergency checklists, shut the engine down, and landed safely at a nearby airport. Had they not been prepared with a solid flight plan, they may not have realized that they had an airport just a few miles away at which to land.

The feeling of preparation gave my friend and his co-pilot a great deal of confidence and mental freedom to handle the rather intense situation of flying the aircraft with only one engine.

Challenges happen to everyone—but they don't have to take you out of commission. Planning is your strength. Planning helps lessen the shock of being taken off guard by a setback or an emergency. Thinking ahead gives you the ability to think about a problem creatively, opening your mind for problem solving and concise decision making.

Where a half-cooked plan leaves you feeling lost in times of challenge, a solid plan provides options.

And here's another thing—nothing can boost your confidence quite like rising to the challenge. When a setback emerges, suddenly and without notice, you can either react or respond.

Reacting is emotional. Responding is logical.

Since you planned for other contingencies, and you feel confident in solving the challenge, your brain is pre-programmed for success because you already handled the other challenges by thinking ahead of the problem.

No matter what happens, you're prepared. And when you're prepared, you're more in control.

The Sonic Boom Of Your Success

What's more important than your life? You might say your kids, spouse, or pets come first. But consider how your own dreams and vision—your purpose—outweighs everything else. If you don't value your own dreams and the vision for your own life above all else then you won't make a difference in the world, let alone the lives of the people you love.

I'm not talking about putting yourself first in a self-serving or inconsiderate way.

You have a responsibility to your family, to your community, and most importantly, to *yourself* to be excellent. You not only deserve success, you have a responsibility to tap the depths of your greatness.

Doubt it? Consider the best thing you've ever accomplished. Maybe it was becoming a parent… starting a business… getting married… saving a life.

Now think about the lives you touched in the process. The children you brought into the world, the employees and clients you serve with your business, the joy you bring to your spouse, the gratitude of the person and their family when you saved that life.

Had you not become who you are today, the world would be a much different place. And the world is a better place when you are connected to your mission and purpose.

Building a solid plan to achieve what you were born to do is not only an inspiring shot to the arm, but your responsibility. When you take on your true purpose and your dreams, you send a shock wave through the world—much like a jet breaking the sound barrier.

Achieving your goals is one thing; going about it in a systematic and logical manner demonstrates to the world that you are a true champion of life. Taking massive, purposeful action towards accomplishing your dream will have a ripple effect across your sphere of influence. Here are just a few effects you will have on the world around you as you plan your journey to your ultimate vision:

» You will demonstrate your commitment to your dreams; in so doing you'll show the people looking up to you what it takes to systematically and purposefully pursue success.

» All the effort in the world means little without focused intention, consistency of action, and inspired commitment—these determine your results and direction. And when you plug into this "zone" of higher performance, you demonstrate a deeper level of excellence.

» You will show that you are a person "on purpose"—
something too few people do nowadays. Give the
world around you something to cheer about as they
see you march toward your dreams with purpose and
confidence.

» One of the greatest joys I have as a success coach is
watching a client connect to their life's purpose, their
"why". Everybody's "why" is different. The size and
scope, the reach and impact of each person's "why" is
personal to them. There is no right or wrong definition. The only part that matters is that you feel *alive*
when you are connected to it. It is the feeling you get
when you are "in the flow" and you seem to execute
with little or no effort, and the hours fly by when you
are doing it.

» When you are working within your "why" you are
working hard; in fact, you may work harder when
connected to your "why" than at any other time in
your life, however you do so without the limitations
and resistance you experience when you do the stuff
you despise. Granted, we all have things we must do
that we really don't love: paying the bills, doing our
taxes, sitting in traffic, going through security at the
airport. That's life, and everyone deals with that kind
of stuff.

» But if your life, your career, your relationships, and
your mind are constantly occupied with frustration
and dissatisfaction, then it is safe to assume you are
not living your "why". Stop living a life full of activities you hate. It is so critical, my friend, to be in love

with what you do. And if you are not, it is time to start looking for that love. You owe it to yourself and the world around you to live by example, to live *your* truth.

» There are a few, basic requirements for discovering and living your "why" fully. First, you must be open to completely and totally loving yourself. Yes, a driven, "Type-A" Naval Aviator just said that. If the idea of loving yourself is a challenge, then please read the next passage with an absolute open mind and heart.

» Until you love yourself enough to gift yourself the freedom to live with passion and joy, you will always short-change yourself. You will accept less than you deserve and allow mediocrity to make a home in your daily life. You cannot honor your true calling without first recognizing your value and worth, and your worthiness to live your dreams.

» It matters not how much money you make or don't make. It matters not how many friends you have or don't have. It matters not how much you lost, gained, tripped over, gave away, celebrated, mourned, squandered or scraped together; if you do not honor and love yourself *first and foremost*, your thirst for success will never be quenched and your gift will never fully be realized.

» But if you choose the courageous path to self-respect, self-love, and self-acceptance, you will accomplish far more than wealth, health, success and attainment. And this is when you begin to connect to your "why". It is through that shift that you open up to the limitless possibilities of what you are capable of, and what you will achieve.

» You will build and exude confidence. When you know where you are going, you'll know when you arrive, and you will have a clear picture of how you are going to get there as you fly your mission in life. You will walk with top-gun confidence. And people will start to back you and support you, because you will live like a champion. And everyone loves a champion.

The Genius Credential

You are a genius. You knew that, right? And no, I'm not being sarcastic… I'm serious.

If that statement makes you wonder, perhaps you're thinking the word "genius" only applies to the likes of Albert Einstein, Beethoven, or Shakespeare.

I was flying a mission with a seasoned co-pilot where we were conducting sonobuoy testing just off the coast of San Diego. Sonobuoys are essentially a string of microphones used to listen for submarines and ships in the water.

Our mission that day was to deploy sonobuoys by dropping them from the belly of our airplane via ballistic charges that shot them into the water.

Flying just a few hundred feet off the water at over 130 miles per hour requires precision and feel. As we approached our drop point, the range supervisor—the person in charge of guiding us through the drop sequences—told us to delay our approach for two minutes by going in a complete circle, then resuming our approach.

My co-pilot, realizing that flying a circle would only take about 90 seconds, opted instead to fly a figure-8 pattern, which put us right on target, right on time.

"Nice move, you're a genius." I said.

"Don't be a smart ass, JT," he responded.

"No, I'm serious! Great call on the figure 8—what made you think to do that?" I asked.

"I don't know," he answered, "it just felt natural, I guess."

Most people assume that "genius" implies only a high IQ or vast amounts of knowledge and education.

Yet the Merriam-Webster Dictionary defines genius as "an attendant spirit of a person or place", "a person who influences another for good or bad" or "a peculiar, distinctive, or identifying character or spirit".

And consider the etymology, or root of the word: from Latin, it means "tutelary spirit and natural inclinations".

In fact, studies have shown that "genius" really comes from a person's ability to access both left brain (the logic side) and right brain (creative side) faculties.

With little margin for error, my co-pilot demonstrated that fact by going with his natural inclinations to adjust to an unusual situation and achieve the desired result.

Your natural inclinations are a powerful indication of your purpose. They also provide you the creative input you need to create your flight plan.

As I can attest, a lifelong vision may be met with opposition. You may have a few people in your corner—or none at all. But that's all the more reason to believe your dream is your birthright; that you deserve to succeed no matter what.

High Altitude Living

Today, more than ever, too many people have given up on their dreams. Many find it easier to make excuses for why it cannot be done instead of how and why it *must* be done. Rarely does anyone start off with all the answers and know-how, but too often, many start off with no plan. While the "flying by the seat of your pants" approach is admirable, it is a poor substitute for forward thinking, vision, and purposeful planning.

Say you have an idea to start a business. You know how to provide value, maybe you even do a little research, get funding, and go. All the while, people you know and trust caution you to "be careful". Even those with whom you've only had casual interactions begin to chime in—warning you of someone they know who once tried, failed, and lost it all.

For the most part, they mean no harm. It's not an insidious plot to get you to fail or keep you stuck where you are; they may be saying these things because they genuinely love and care about you. But instead of helping, they're planting seeds of doubt and despair.

Then you launch—and perhaps you fail. Not only does it hurt, but you're faced with looks of *I told you so*. Friends and family may offer a shoulder to cry on, an ear to bitch to, maybe even a "pep talk": *not everyone is meant to do big things*. Casual acquaintances treat you as the big pink elephant in the room. It sucks.

With no plan, it's easy to lose your bearings under such circumstances.

However, with a plan in place you have a reference point to begin again—rerouting procedures, as it were. Sure, you still have the naysayers... the concerned looks... maybe even the whisperings behind your back. But you also have a reminder of where you're coming from—and where you want to go.

High-Speed, Low-Drag Thinking

When you look at the design of high speed aircraft—whether a fighter jet or the more advanced business jets—it's easy to see how they can efficiently fly at high speeds.

Gone are the multi-surface designs of the biplanes and gliders from the dawn of aviation. Today's aircraft are sleeker, faster, and more maneuverable because unnecessary parts that previously caused drag and loss of airspeed have been eliminated.

The same refinement of your approach to achieving your dreams is necessary for a smoother flight to success.

A well calculated plan always runs smoother. Let's face it: when you have a clear vision of where you want to go, when you want to arrive, and an explicit, step-by-step plan for doing so, you don't spend as much mental energy executing the plan.

When we planned flights in the Navy, there was always a tendency to want to over-think the problem, rather than focus on the solution or the outcome. Everyone from brand new rookies to seasoned vets would get wrapped around minute details in an effort to make the mission flow more smoothly. At first blush, this seems prudent, but if overdone, this can be a death sentence for productivity.

And we do it all the time in our own lives—either over thinking the problem—or thinking it's more trouble than it's worth.

Proper planning will help keep you on track if you keep the following in mind:

Plan your mission;

Evaluate the plan;

Execute the plan;

Refine your processes as you go.

Plan, evaluate, execute, refine—and don't over think.

You will always make course corrections along your path to success—just as an airplane must steer into shifting winds in order to stay on course.

Too often, people feel they have to plan every last detail, every possible contingency plan, and have all the answers before taking off on their journey.

The fact is that you won't have all the answers; you won't have all the "what ifs" thought through. In fact, we often gain far more wisdom from taking inspired, yet imperfect action; we discover what works and what doesn't. Massive, inspired, yet imperfect action is far more effective than dotting all the "I's" and crossing all the "T's" in an attempt to get it right before we start.

Ultimately, you'll make several small corrections along your flight path, and those corrections, guided by your inner genius, will be imperative to getting your desired results

The key is to have a solid plan built, take some time to think critically about it before executing, but then *execute* with inspired, yet imperfect action.

Putting In The Legwork

Even pilots, at times, loathe the flight planning process because it's tedious or boring.

Perhaps you can relate.

Will it be hard at times? Probably. Will it suck every now and again? Most likely. Will you doubt yourself—feel inadequate, confused, embarrassed, unprepared, and discouraged? Almost certainly. But any worthwhile goal requires a lot of work. And if it pushes you, and brings out a little fear, that's a good indication that you're on to something big.

A rule of thumb for setting a goal and backing it with your vision: be unreasonable in your dreams, but pragmatic in your approach.

To get yourself through the tedium, remember:

It won't always be easy; but then the really amazing things in life rarely come on a silver platter. Plan, commit, execute, and persist. It may take longer than you first thought, and you'll likely work harder than you imagined you would have to, but the results of living your mission are well worth the commitment and sacrifices along the way.

It may be hard, confusing—even clumsy. You may start off feeling like a fish out of water, struggling to make even the slightest bit of headway. But this is typical when undertaking a significant task, particularly if you have never tried it before. Hang in there. Don't get discouraged. Being good at something takes time. Mastering it takes a lifetime.

It may seem like a bad idea after the initial adrenaline wears off. This is typical. I remember after the first few weeks of flight school—after the novelty wore off, drudgery set in. Everything seemed harder. I had to keep my long-term "why" of becoming a Blue Angel in mind in order to fend off the frustrations of flight school. Remind yourself that you are going for something big, something important, and how very few people in this world have the courage to put themselves out there like you are doing right now.

Our brains are actually engineered to keep us safe, and to sense danger in order to limit our effort. Some studies indicate that 20% of our total energy is consumed by our brains. In an effort to preserve itself, our brain sends us messages to "pull back" and conserve energy. This is how we can get sucked into the false feeling of pushing too far and therefore start "playing it safe", but we are physically and mentally capable of far more than we can imagine. It's in our biology to want to hold back and play it safe.

You probably will not die, but if you do, you died in pursuit of your grandest dream. This may seem a little extreme—but some people have made an addictive habit of blowing things way out of proportion. Often times through no fault of their own, a person will perceive growth as a step closer to death. The fear of moving beyond a comfort zone can be deathly frightening. The good news is you probably won't die. But, if you die in pursuit of your life's big dream, that is not a bad way to go.

And remember: *You are tougher and more capable than you think.*

Write that on sticky notes and place them throughout your home, car, on your computer, in your office, and on your pillow. The human body and human spirit are amazing in what they can endure. The sad reality is that most people quit at the first sign of pain. When given the opportunity to either avoid pain or gain pleasure, people are hardwired to opt for the avoidance of pain. Push yourself beyond your comfort zone. Pain doesn't last, but champions do.

Flight planning is the little thing you can do to ensure success in a massive endeavor, even before it gets off the ground. And you do it, not because it's easy or fun—but because it helps ensure a safe arrival at your destination.

Flying Above Fear And Uncertainty

I will never forget the flight home from my first deployment as a rookie pilot. Rookies are referred to as "nuggets", and on this flight, we were leaving our base on a small atoll in the Indian Ocean and flying back to the United States after our combat deployment in support of Operation Enduring Freedom.

The entire base was enshrouded in enormous thunderstorms that reached into the stratosphere. The rain pelted down, the sky was pitch black, and the only thing that made the flight at all desirable was that it would ultimately conclude back home in the States. To add to the urgency, we had a severely injured sailor and his medical support staff aboard. We were to drop the sailor and medical team off at a medical facility on the other side of the Indian Ocean as we progressed toward home.

As we took the runway, lightning, thunder, and torrential rain hammered the aircraft. I have to admit that I was *not* brimming with confidence as we stared down the gaping mouth of the monstrous storm!

We applied full power and the plane lurched forward into the dismal storm. As we climbed, all hell broke loose.

Turbulence slammed the aircraft and knocked cargo from its moorings. Static electricity caused the front windscreen panels to glow an eerie black and blue static like a television that had lost its signal, a phenomenon referred to as "St. Elmo's Fire". I looked over my shoulder out the side windows to witness our wings literally flapping in the turbulence and heavy winds.

"Nice night!" my co-pilot shouted over the noise. "Yeah... awesome," I yelled, trying to sound like I was enjoying it all. I could envision the wing being ripped clean off the fuselage, and the thunderstorm slamming us into the murky ocean below.

Then, after fifteen minutes of our departure from the base, almost suddenly everything went calm. The night sky was brilliantly illuminated by the moon and dazzling stars. The noise and chaos had ended. We had finally penetrated the storm and reached calm, smooth air.

I was amazed at the resilience of the aircraft—packed full of fuel, gear, and weary warriors—how it managed to weather the storm and climb undaunted to smooth air above. I cannot count how many times during those first fifteen minutes I wanted to turn around and head back to base. Those moments were frightening—they were tough.

But the aircraft—and the crew—were tougher. We rose above the challenge to the clear skies above.

So it must be with you. While the storms of doubt and fear may encircle you just as you prepare to take off toward your dreams, understand that you have what it takes to climb above it all—and your Flight Plan to Success™ is all you need to make it happen.

Getting Back On Course

Your life doesn't have to be in shambles to be off course; you can be slightly off without you ever knowing it—until that one or two degrees deviation ends with you being hundreds of miles off course from your dreams and goals.

The end of your flight—with fuel nearly exhausted—is not the time to realize you had been ignoring the warnings signs all along. Stay focused on the desired result, and take note of when you are straying off course. It's easier to make smaller adjustments early, than monumental corrections at the end of the journey.

Life is the same way. We're only gifted with a certain amount of time to reach our ultimate destination until the fuel of life runs out. Our ultimate destination is our true purpose, our calling.

So begin with a solid strategy for building a plan—your flight plan—to visualize, prepare for, and execute your dreams and success. And in the next chapter, we'll uncover the basic tools you'll need to begin creating and executing your Flight Plan To Success™.

☑ Flight Plan Checklist

Define your burning desires, your goals, and your dreams.

☐ Specify exactly why those aspirations are important to you. How will they affect your future? How will they impact your family, friends, community, and world as a whole?

☐ Why will you accomplish your dreams? Why are your dreams bigger and more powerful than your previous excuses?

☐ What are some new strategies you can use to monitor your progress and stay on course to your dreams?

Describe setbacks you have encountered in the past, and how having your flight plan in place will assist you in breaking through those barriers.

CHAPTER 2

LAYING THE FOUNDATION FOR YOUR FLIGHT PLAN

When a pilot wants to fly over long distances, in questionable weather, or where air traffic control (ATC) service is provided, he files a flight plan. This complex process involves the pilot submitting a written description of the pilot's intentions to a local ATC facility, which, in turn, enables ATC not only to track the pilot, but all aircraft, at any given time—thus scheduling and separating traffic and helping to ensure safe arrivals for all flights.

Both ATC and the pilot keep a copy of the flight plan on hand during the flight. This allows ATC to watch the aircraft on its radar system and the pilot to monitor his own progress as he approaches his destination.

A flight plan not only outlines the journey, but it also gives the pilot crystal clarity on how to get from point "A" to point "B".

You need a similar approach to your goals.

Goals are good, but they mean nothing if they aren't backed by vision. Vision is to goals what gold is to currency; it makes them legitimate. Vision defines the goals and gives them that critical ingredient necessary to achieve them—significance.

When it comes to your personal mission, you don't need to plan every aspect of your life down to the minute. But you do need to plan.

So take a few hours—perhaps even a few days—and focus on exactly where you want to go and how you're going to get there.

And I'll show you how to build your Flight Plan To Success™ right now.

Be Clear And Respond vs. React

Whenever I flew with a solid flight plan in my hands, I had the confidence of knowing my crew and I had thought through the mission before takeoff. We knew how much fuel our aircraft had, how long we could fly with that fuel; we knew the distance to each checkpoint and possible divert airfields along the way should we need to make an emergency landing. We knew all this and more before we ever set foot in the airplane.

The fact that we had already done the thinking about those issues before they were ever a factor freed our minds to consider possible solutions to any challenge thrown our way. It gave us more mental freedom to come up with excellent options for a successful outcome to our mission. A mission could not be scrapped just because of a simple system malfunction with the aircraft or an unforeseen challenge along the route of flight.

This is why you must have a concise plan before you execute on your goal.

Using Your GPS

In the early days of flight, pilots relied on line-of-sight navigation to fly to their destinations. Even today, flying Visual Flight Rules (VFR)—using visual landmarks and special charts to navigate over the ground—is common practice.

While this technique has been around as long as manned flight, it has its limitations. Flying at night or in foul weather, for instance, is a challenge, and long distance flying of this nature can really drain the pilot physically and mentally. Also, flying at high altitude is not only limited, but above certain altitudes pilots are required to fly with an Instrument Flight Rules (IFR) flight plan and use their instruments and navigation equipment to execute the mission.

One piece of gear that has become a staple in just about every advanced aircraft is the GPS, or Global Positioning System. The concept behind a GPS is that a receiver onboard the aircraft collects input from satellites high above the earth's surface. These signals triangulate, or pinpoint, the aircraft's position over the ground. Depending on the number of satellites and the GPS's calibration, the pilot can get extremely accurate readings of their location.

The GPS can also be loaded with points along the intended route so the pilot can gauge how accurate his or her track is over the intended route of flight.

In order for a GPS to work effectively, it requires two points: the desired destination and its starting position. The pilot must input the exact location of the destination or target. Naturally, this location is dictated by the mission. Secondly, the GPS must know the exact location from which it is beginning the mission in order to calculate and create the most accurate flight plan possible.

In the aircraft I flew in the Navy, the GPS systems we used required up to 15 minutes to calculate this exact starting position. It was imperative that we not move the aircraft until this calculation, called "initializing", was complete. If we were to taxi to the runway, let alone take to the skies and go flying, before this initialization phase was complete, we could be several miles dangerously off course as a result of confusion on the part of our GPS.

Just like high altitude flight, you require a GPS for your pursuits in life. If you intend to go high places, then you must utilize your own GPS, which stands for:

Goal

Purpose

Strategy

One challenge I have with traditional goal-setting is there is very little process in place. The same old regurgitated theory uses words like "specific", "measurable", "attainable" and expects you to build a purpose-built life around that. Sure, this theory has worked for many in the past, but it is outdated at best. When the Ford Model A first was introduced in 1903, it topped out at 28 miles per hour, which was breakneck speed at that time. Today, cars like the Lamborghini Aventador LP-700 reaches speeds of nearly 220 miles per hour. If I challenged you to a coast-to-coast race and offered you either the Model A or the Lamborghini, which would you chose? Traditional goal-setting practices are like that Model A; let me introduce you to the Lamborghini of success and achievement.

The first major deficiency with traditional goal setting is that you are told to set your goals, get really specific, really "feel" them, and then go get 'em! In that model, 100% of the time, energy and focus is placed on the goal. In reality, your actual goal is less important than *why* you want it. The purpose of the goal is way more important than what it is, however *being clear on what you want is absolutely critical.*

So how do we set better goals? Let's begin with the equation:

Success = GPS

We all have our own definitions for what success is, what it means, what it looks like, and how it feels. So I challenge you right now to answer these questions:

» What is your definition of success?

» How does success look, feel, sound, and taste to you?

» *Why* is that (your vision of success) so important to you; important enough to go all-in and do whatever it takes to make it a reality?

» What does that feeling—the feeling of success— represent to you? Freedom? Love? Joy? Fulfillment? Contribution?

If you are unsure about how to answer these questions, start with your core values. Your core values drive nearly every decision, every thought, every opinion, and every action you take. For a complimentary exercise to help you nail this down with crystal clarity, got to www.FlightPlanToSuccess .com/GPS for an awesome tool I've put together to help you gain clarity on this.

Once you've defined what success means, you can use the rest of the equation to begin building your Flight Plan To Success™ and move forward.

Here's an exercise you can do in your journal. Above the letter "G" in "GPS" write the number 5. Above the letter "P", write the number 70. And above the letter "S" write the number 25. These are the percentages to assign the time, energy and focus to the three components of your Success GPS.

For the "G" of Goal-definition, invest 5% of your time, energy and focus. Dream big, get clear, and make this your own.

For the "P" of Purpose, invest 70% of your time, energy and focus. This is the backbone of your success. All the specificity, measurability, attainability, etc. of your goal means nothing without rock-solid purpose. As a coach, I'm less intrigued by what you want as I am by *why* you want it. And here is another distinction to make: don't make this a want, make it a *must*. When you shift your focus in this way, you become a force to be reckoned with. You become unstoppable.

Finally, for the "S" in Strategy, invest 25% of your time, energy and focus in the "how". How you do it is not as critical as why; but it is crucial to your success. We will begin working on your strategy in the next chapter.

I love doing this work with my clients; for many, this is their first experience getting down deep on what they truly want, *why* they want it, and what it truly *means* to them.

Too often, we try to fly "line-of-sight" to our goals instead of listening to our own internal GPS. Be clear on what you want, why you want it, and then build the strategy to get there. And remember the importance of the initialization phase of the aircraft GPS; it applies to yours as well.

Investing the time in getting clear—and getting real—with where you currently are in relation to your dreams and goals in crucial for long-term success. I'm always surprised when a client comes to me wanting better results in business or life, and they have avoided taking a long, hard look in the mirror of reality. It's not always fun, but it is rarely as bad as you initially think it will be. But it is the only way to know your exact starting point on the flight path to your dreams.

For example, if your dream is to have a million dollars in the bank one year from today, your strategy will be far different if you are starting with $25,000 as opposed to $250,000. And the deeper questions revolve around your attitudes and mindset surrounding your dreams. Where is your belief level? What are your expectations? This is what I mean when I encourage you to get clear on the starting point of your mission.

Accommodating Change

It's common for flight plans to change during flights. This happens due to changes in weather patterns, unexpected air traffic, fuel requirements, or aircraft malfunctions. Since things do happen, having a solid plan for a desired outcome allows both pilot and ATC to work in concert to ensure a successful mission.

More than likely, your personal flight plan will also change. The important thing is to remain true to your mission. Don't give up. Being flexible and thinking creatively is paramount in overcoming obstacles and barriers to success.

If you fail and keep failing—maybe it's time to take a look at your mission with a fresh approach. With a solid plan in place you can respond with logic-based troubleshooting versus emotion-driven reaction to challenges and setbacks. You can say, "Well, that didn't work. But *this* could work instead." You go into the endeavor with an emboldened sense of confidence, and that confidence acts as a foundation for the attitude you'll carry through the entire mission.

Focusing In On Your Mission - 5%

Living with purpose is one of the key components to success and happiness. A flight plan begins with a mission. Your mission will begin with goals—aspirations for your life.

Think of your most recurring idea or aspiration—the one that comes to you often, and don't be afraid to dream big.

It may be the one that hits you in the middle of the night and rattles you out of a restful sleep. Perhaps it's the distracting thought that can't be shaken—a secret desire you've always wanted to pursue. It may even be something you've done before that brought total bliss, like sports, art, music, or a civic activity, and very likely it is something you loved as a kid back when everything was possible and before the burdens of adulthood beat it down.

There's a reason you have a natural tendency toward certain things. This just may be your true calling.

Once you understand your natural tendencies, take the time to assess the reason you navigate toward them.

What are the things you love to do—hobbies, pastimes, activities and your passions in life? What do you do effortlessly? What would you do without pay for the rest of your life because you love it so much? Now, how do those things (or that one thing) fit into your dreams and vision of your life?

Once you have a clear picture of the things you love, the ways you go about enjoying them, and perhaps even an idea of how you could incorporate them into your life as the main fixture of your time, you will begin to have a sharper picture of what your mission can and should be.

Assigning Purpose - 70%

No pilot worth his salt would preflight an aircraft without a flight plan, let alone fly into the great unknown without a solid purpose.

Take a look at your dreams and goals— your mission. To make the journey worthwhile, you must define your purpose—why do you want to endure the mission? Why do you want to arrive at the final destination?

Pretty pictures and motivational quotes mean little without purpose.

You must tie your goals to a purpose higher than the surface reasons—and the stronger your purpose, the stronger your resolve. The stronger your resolve, the more likely you will succeed regardless of the size and scope of your dreams.

If your goal is to become a millionaire by your birthday next year, define exactly why that is so important. Is it just about the money? If so, you may be in for frustration. But if you desire to become a millionaire to ensure an excellent quality of life for your family, to make an impact on your community, or give freely to your favorite charity, then you will have much more resolute purpose for going after that challenge.

Most achievers are busy today and feel they don't have time to assess what drives them, what stokes their inner fire. But why would you want to fly into the skies of uncertainty without a clear flight plan of where you're going in life and *why* you're headed that way?

Once you've set very specific goals for your life—you've focused in on a mission and understand the higher purpose for achieving success—it's time to implement powerful strategies for achieving them.

☑ Flight Plan Checklist

Define your genius: what are your natural inclinations? What inspires you to think bigger, act more passionately, and strive for a more significant life?

☐ Set yourself up for success: what are some of the challenges you foresee coming up along your flight path? How might you grow so as to respond, and avoid reacting?

☐ Calibrate your GPS: what are your vision-backed goals? What is your purpose for going after them? What is your current situation relative to your dreams and your vision?

☐ What dreams and aspirations keep nudging you and begging for attention? What contributions would you make to the world if money were no object?

☐ Based on your natural inclinations, what would you love to do for the rest of your life, even if you didn't get paid to do it? Now, what are some ways you could monetize your passions?

CHAPTER 3

THE FLIGHT PLAN TO SUCCESS™

Now that you know how to create and calibrate your GPS, it's time to build your strategy: your Flight Plan To Success™. Building your flight plan requires more than plotting your destination and starting point. Planning out the course you'll fly requires thinking through contingencies, marshaling the resources you'll need, and defining the time and date of the completion of your mission.

I have the privilege of working with individuals and organizations around the world on their strategies. It's inspiring to see the shift of momentum that occurs as these committed people get clear, get focused and get going with a rock-solid strategy that helps them efficiently and consistently hit their targets in business and life.

Why then, don't more people invest the time and attention into planning their biggest dreams and missions, then go for it full speed ahead?

Part of this is rooted in fear. The fear of failure; that they may dream big only to come up short of the finish line and be judged on the lack of results. Fear of success; the fear that if they succeed, they'll have to live up to a new expectation and standard that they may not see themselves capable of sustaining. And the fear of loss; not only losing what they earned, but losing the friends and family and people that occupy their current circles of influence.

But perhaps the deeper issue is they fear that they don't have what it takes to succeed—the talent, resources, know-how or endurance to see their dream all the way through to completion. And the sad fact is that in most cases, these fears are often only false perceptions and rarely ever realized. Perhaps you may even harbor fears like these.

There are endless excuses we give ourselves for why something can't be done. Too often, we feel limited by what we see right in front of us. Either through a lack of imagination, a forgetful mind, or simply being so focused on the task at hand, we miss solutions in the face of challenges or frustrations. To achieve success sometimes you must look past the obvious.

But here's a simple fact: *you have everything you need to accomplish anything you want.*

Read that sentence again. There are two critical words to focus on as you take the message onboard. The first is *everything*. You have *everything* you need to accomplish anything you want; the key is being clear on what you need and then taking the action to get access to it. This is not to say it will be easy or obvious.

You may have to work harder than you think, for longer than you imagine. You may have to be more creative than you've ever been to make it happen, but everything you need is currently available to you when you apply focused effort, surround yourself with excellent people, ask the right questions, keep your mind, body, and soul tuned in to the possibilities, and stay vigilant for opportunity.

The second critical word is *anything*; you have everything you need to accomplish *anything* you want. This is your permission to dream and think big. To pursue the dreams you've always wanted with passion and purpose. Forget what others have told you is possible or "right" for you. Dream *your* dream. Accomplish anything *you* want.

Dream the biggest dream you can imagine, and take some time to think of all it would take to make it happen. You'll likely find everything falls into one of four categories, something I call TMAP: Time, Money, Assets, People.

These resources are all around you.

Yes, in the end it still depends on you to make your dream reality. But you can rest in the fact that your world—despite your current situation—can literally provide all you need to succeed.

Recognizing Your Resources

As stated earlier, your resources will more or less fall into the four basic categories of Time, Money, Assets, and People. Consider their correlation to the key elements in aviation:

Time is like altitude: the more you have, the longer you will fly toward your dreams.

Money is like jet fuel: the more you have, the more options you have in order to reach your destination.

Assets are like your aircraft: the kind of assets you have will dictate the type of mission you will fly.

People are your flight crew: pilots are not the only people credited for mission accomplishment; it takes a dedicated team of professionals to ensure the mission is a success. Success is a team sport, and the degree to which you succeed is in direct proportion to the caliber of people with whom you surround yourself.

This list is bookended with the two most important resources—time and people. They hold the key to how far you go and how fast you get there.

Give Yourself Lots Of Excellent Options

The challenge with filling the categories of time, money, assets, and people is we tend to think of one or two examples of each and stop there. The fallacy of that practice is that if one or both options fall through, we scramble to find solutions rather than completing the mission.

I'd like to suggest a different approach. Let's start with the end result in mind—and then list at least five examples of the resources for each category of TMAP.

Five examples of time that, once planned out, begin to bring the dream closer to reality. This could mean scheduling the five (or more) days per week you work on your dream, for instance.

Money: What are five different income streams you can access to finance your dream? This could be income from employment or a business, savings accounts, a piece of cash-flowing real estate, dividends paid from investments, it could even include the simplest cash streams like the revenue from a garage sale, etc.

Assets: What equipment do you need? This list could go on forever, and probably will right up until the time you execute on the goal. Think of it as a laundry list of must-have items to achieve your goals. Give yourself free reign to jot down anything you feel might be crucial for your success, just be sure to list at least 5 most important things you need to make the dream a reality.

People: When it comes to people, there is no more precious a resource in your life. As best-selling author Jack Canfield says, "We are the average of the five people we hang out with the most!" Again, only list the five people who can assist you in achieving your dream. Maybe they're experts in your chosen field; maybe they are financiers, or perhaps they're vital to the execution of the plan. These are people at or above your competence level; people that will push you to succeed. They will comprise the team that will help you get to where you want to go—and chances are, at some point or another, you'll do the same for them.

Beginning With The Destination In Mind

Let me share with you a powerful strategy for achieving your goals and accomplishing your big missions in life. It starts with defining your target with crystal clarity, then working your way backward from success. Whether flying missions in peacetime or in war, or launching your dream, one of the best strategies for accomplishing the mission is by planning your path to success by working backward.

This also served me when I was deployed to Iraq in 2006, this time in a non-flying status. As a military pilot working in conjunction with civilian contractors to rebuild Iraq's oil infrastructure, I felt like a fish out of water. I went from high-flying operations of combat surveillance and reconnaissance to helping plan major overhauls and reconstruction projects of Iraq's oil fields that had been destroyed by years of warfare.

Completing these complicated projects and their many intricate sub-projects took a great deal of planning and forward thinking. My team and I literally had to plan from project completion, backward.

You can use this same technique when planning your biggest missions, from major life and business events to family vacations. And once you've learned how to do this, you'll find it applicable to major projects in your business and life.

Here's how it works:

1. Define your goal.

Set a specific date when you intend to achieve your goal.

3. List your TMAP requirements—Time, Money, Assets and People

4. Write down the 5-10 critical steps required to accomplish the mission. The key here is that you do not have to know every step in order to launch your mission. You are simply brainstorming and listing the critical steps that, to your current knowledge, will be necessary for mission success. Begin with the final action you will need to accomplish prior to completing your goal—then write

down the step before that, and the step before that, and the step before that and so on, until you walk your way back to where you are beginning from right now, today.

While it does take a little imagination, the best way to see the goal is to envision it before it happens. It puts a spin on the old saying of *I'll believe it when I see it*, and rephrases it to the way success really works: *I'll see it when I believe it*.

Here's why it's important: when you decide to do something big—and my guess is you're reading this book because you're on a path to accomplish your biggest dreams in life—the mission can seem daunting at first.

But when you imagine what you'll need to do just before you achieve your goal—and the next action, followed by the next action—in less time than it takes you to make a list of excuses why you can't do it, you'll start to have a clear understanding of how you *will* do it. Your belief will begin to grow.

Here's why this method is so effective: when you begin the process with success in mind *first*, you're literally creating that success by visualizing and planning for the desired outcome, as opposed to getting caught up on the sometimes painful and awkward beginning stages. If you've ever experienced the futility of New Year's resolutions, you can likely relate to this.

Let's take a typical New Year's resolution: getting in shape. The idea of going from soft-and-squishy to fit-and-sexy seems like a great idea until you realize what it entails:

» Clearing out the cupboards of all the comfy food that put the weight on in the first place;

» buying new workout clothes and signing up for a gym membership;

» going to the gym and stumbling through exercises you haven't done in forever (if ever!);

» and feeling sore, stiff and beat up for a week or two as you work your way to fitness.

Sound like fun? No wonder over 70% of New Year's resolutions fail before January 20!

The important part of this process, and one main reason why it is so powerful is the way it opens up your creative mind to finding solutions and answers before they manifest in reality. Think of it as the "what if" method. Asking "what if" gets the brain rolling down the best track for finding solutions. NASA didn't put Apollo 11 on the moon by beginning with, "What kind of launch pad should we build?" or "What color should the astronauts' suits be?" They likely started with a question like, "What if we could get a man on the moon...and back, safely?"

You can use this same method for planning and accomplishing your own missions.

Example:

Let's say your mission is to buy a home in San Diego, California ...

Step I: Define your goal.

To do this, answer some important questions:

What you want: a new home, with number of rooms, square footage, amenities, etc.

Where you want it: San Diego, CA , and include the specific neighborhood and address.

Why this dream is so important to you: this is where you want to raise your family.

Step II: Set a specific date when you intend to achieve your goal.

Step III: Starting with the answer to Step II, walk your way *backward* to where you are today.

Move in on [exact date] → schedule movers → sign final contracts → close escrow → offer accepted → make offer → decide on a specific home → tour home → schedule meeting with realtor → secure funding → decide to buy a new home in San Diego, CA

Step IV: List all mission-essential requirements: TMAP.

How much *time* will it take to research properties, contact realtors, tour the homes, secure funding, etc.?

*IMPORTANT: Set dates on the individual steps you outlined in Step III.

How much *money* do you need (down payment, closing costs, etc)? Where is the money coming from? What additional streams of income must you tap?

What *assets* will help your vision come to life? Things like moving equipment, hotel reservations, travel requirements, etc?

Who are the five most important *people* who will contribute to the attainment of your goal? This is your power team— your flight crew—that will help you find, fund, and move into your dream home.

Other steps to consider:

» Refine the flight plan: look for areas where an extra step will be needed, or an erroneous step can be removed to keep you on track.

» Brief the mission: get together with your support crew—either individually or as a team. Let them know how critical this mission is to your life, and how much you appreciate their contributions. Let each of them know what their specific roles will be, what you expect of them, and what they can expect of you.

When high-altitude people hear your well thought-out plan, and understand the deadlines and destinations, they will be focused and ready to back you up the entire way.

You now have the basic architecture of your Flight Plan To Success™. From here you can begin structuring the actual path from where you stand today, to where (and whom) you want to be tomorrow.

Preparing For Flight

The key to executing a solid flight plan is having your resources lined up and ready to go, or at least thought through and considered before you takeoff toward your goal. Don't sell yourself short with only one or two options for each category; be sure you have excellent *and* appropriate options in the event the need arises to call upon them, especially in the category of people.

And if the resources are not immediately available, keep the faith. Just know when the chips seem down or when you think you've run out of all options, as long as you have prepared yourself and done the ground work, mighty forces seem to magically appear and come to your aid. When they do, you need to be ready.

To get a better understanding of the role of these resources, let's delve a little deeper into each. And what better place to start than with the resource that is perhaps the most misunderstood and underappreciated: Time.

☑ Flight Plan Checklist

What kinds of resources and assets do you require to make your dream a reality?

☐ How specifically do those assets and resources fit into your overall mission? What roles do they perform in the achievement of your dream?

☐ How much money, in an exact amount, will you need to realize your dream? How will you acquire it?

☐ Who are the key people that come to mind that you will reach out to in order to achieve your dream? What specific roles do you need them to fill?

Make a definitive plan to begin organizing the TMAP structure for your flight plan.

CHAPTER 4

TIME: THE ALTITUDE OF YOUR SUCCESS

Jet fuel and altitude have a very close relationship in aviation. When I first started flight school, I was performing a pre-flight inspection by walking around the plane, checking various components prior to a training flight. As I inspected the blades of the propeller, my flight instructor asked, "What is that?"

"…well it's the propeller, Sir," I said, not knowing where he was going with his line of questioning.

"No, Ensign…that's the air conditioner."

"Sir?" I said with confusion in my voice.

"Yeah. Because when that thing stops spinning, you'll start sweating! Get strapped in…"

While I never ran out of fuel in my military flight career, I did shut down engines in flight for training and fuel conservation—common practice for the P-3 Orion, the aircraft I flew for the bulk of my flight career. And no matter how many times a pilot performs these routine procedures, there's always something a little unnatural about *intentionally* shutting down your source of propulsion in flight.

Yes, if you run out of fuel, and have plenty of altitude, you can glide long enough to find a suitable place to land. However, if you run out of altitude and have plenty of fuel, you stand a good chance of creating a spectacular fireball upon impact with the terrain.

Utilizing time can accelerate your flight plan to help you reach higher altitudes. Learn the strategies for leveraging your time—for using it to your ultimate advantage—and begin to accomplish more than you ever thought possible.

Just as altitude correlates to time, the better you handle your time, the further you'll fly in business and life. And we'll discuss some ways you can maximize the time you have.

Why Time Is The Most Valuable Asset

A common misconception is that money is the most vital resource when it comes to success and achievement. In the next chapter, we'll discuss how, like jet fuel, money is a critical component to mission success. While money is important, it is not the be-all-end-all as many people think. In fact, if you consider the fact that money is made of paper, and paper is made of trees, then money actually *does* grow on trees!

If you are short on cash, you can generate more of it if you have enough time. In fact, within a very short amount of time, you can generate enough money to live the rest of your life on your terms. But time does not grow on trees; in fact, all the money in the world cannot buy back a single moment of time.

Even with that said, it is easy to allow our time to be robbed from us on a daily basis. Intrusions on our time come in the form of email, social media, phone calls, visits from friends, family, colleagues, and social commitments, the agendas of others, errands—you name it. With our seemingly never-ending "to-do" lists and ability to be reached by almost anyone at anytime, it is no wonder our time is at a premium, now more than ever. And it is of little surprise that in this chaotic environment, our dreams and goals begin to take a backseat to the tyranny of urgency.

Always guard your time and remember: time is not a luxury, it's an asset. Invest it wisely.

Moving Closer To Your Dream

Now is the time to place top priority on the implementation of your flight plan. Your dreams, from here on out, must take priority in your life. Do not mistake what I am saying here; friends, family, and health come above all else. But if you do not place your dreams and goals in an appropriate place of respect and focus, you risk neglecting them and paying severe consequences that even money cannot correct.

Don't be lulled into the deception that you'll "get to it later". This is one of the biggest dream killers in the world. We're blessed with a finite amount of time. There is no guarantee that tomorrow will come. And even if you knew you would live another 100 years, why would you waste any more time hoping for the day your dream can come true? Jump in and start pursuing your dream today; live with passion and purpose every day.

When you invest your time in the pursuit of your dream, you're doing your most important work. First, by focusing on your dream, by doing something as simple as researching and learning more about it—you're literally moving closer to it.

Secondly, your investment of time in your dream enables you to find new ways to make it a reality. As you focus on the goal, and make a regular habit of working toward it every day, it possesses a place front and center in your consciousness. Your brain begins to recognize opportunities and resources that will enable you to efficiently accomplish your goal.

When you invest your most precious asset of time, your brain associates value to your goals. Instead of it being some flight of fancy, it becomes a weighted, important, consuming priority. It may ultimately turn into a healthy obsession.

The example you set for others to follow simply by respecting, valuing, and investing your time wisely will set the tone for the rest of your life. Not only does your brain take on a new level of respect for your dreams, but so does the rest of your world. The people in your life will begin to understand just how solid your purpose is, and more readily jump to your aid when you call upon them.

Consistently investing time in the pursuit of your dreams and the construction of your flight plan will dictate how far you go in the achievement of all your dreams.

Understanding The Importance Of Time

Time is the least understood, and therefore often the least respected asset we have. Recognizing its importance and utilizing it to move you closer to your true vision is critical.

If you drop twenty dollars on the street, you can get it back in minutes—maybe even seconds. But you forever lose twenty minutes of your life by watching television, checking email, or updating your status on social media!

Instead of sitting in front of the television watching other people live their dreams, get up and start working on *your* dream. Respect yourself, respect your dreams and invest your time wisely.

In order to plan your time efficiently and appropriately, you must first respect it. Once you have a full respect for time, squandering it becomes less of an issue.

Prepare Like A Pilot: Altitude Equals Time

In most cases, a pilot files a flight plan to land at a certain destination and ends up there safe and sound. Other times, a mechanical malfunction or weather-related setback may force the pilot to land unexpectedly at a different airport than the desired destination. And, in very rare cases, a pilot may even be forced to make an emergency landing anywhere they can—a road, an open field, even out at sea.

Because of this, throughout a pilot's career—from initial flight training to proficiency flights—pilots train to fly their aircraft in almost any emergency situation.

An example of this is the critical maneuver practiced on just about every training flight: engine failure. In the event of a total loss of engine power, pilots must be adept at maneuvering their aircraft without the thrust provided by their engines. With no engines to power the aircraft, they glide. Gravity takes over and supplies the energy needed to create the airspeed that provides the lift.

The challenge with an engine failure is that altitude is finite. And the time available to find a suitable place to land is determined by how far the pilot can glide the plane with no engine power.

Understanding how far a plane will glide without power, and how much altitude is lost in the glide is crucial for success in an "engine-out" scenario.

Altitude in that case literally equals time. The higher you are from the ground, the more time you have before you reach it.

That altitude-to-time translation is crucial. It allows the pilot time to assess the malfunction, take corrective action, radio for help, and if necessary, find a suitable place to land the crippled craft.

There's a saying in aviation, "Any landing you can walk away from is a good landing." In other words, you do whatever you have to in order to live to fly another day.

Even a crash landing—while seen by most as a failure—is a success provided everyone lives to fly again.

The higher you fly, the more time you have to stay in the game. As you fly your way toward your dream, make sure you're flying at a high enough altitude to give yourself the options you need to ensure success. We're talking about maximizing your time.

Gaining Altitude, Maximizing Time

Taking time to focus on your dream requires a concerted effort. Block out a set period of time everyday to invest in your dream. If you're a morning person, get up earlier to spend time focused on your vision before your day starts. If you're a night person, stay up an hour later.

This should be dedicated, focused time. Your work area should be as free of distractions as possible. No cell phones, television, email, bills, or issues unrelated to your goal.

Here's a simple checklist to assist you in making quality time to create and execute your Flight Plan To Success™:

Schedule extra time. Make sure you allot for time to get up and running in the morning or wind down at night.

Morning people: wake up early enough to allot for at least a full hour of dedicated focus to your mission.

Evening people: stay up an hour or more later; sacrifice television and do this after dedicating quality time to your family.

Champions: wake up an hour earlier *and* stay up an hour later

Dedicate work space. Assign a specific location such as a home office, a library, or a private study area for working on your vision—a place where you will not be interrupted, where you can truly focus on the task at hand. Place pictures and reminders of your vision where you can see them. If this sounds corny to you, I totally understand, but hear me out. Pilots use visualization just as Olympic athletes do. We do an exercise called "chair flying". This is where we sit in a chair, and go through the motions of flying complex maneuvers. I even used to walk around my coffee table in the living room of my house to "practice" doing touch-and-go landings. My performance in the cockpit improved dramatically. Use visualization to train your brain to live your dreams even before they materialize. Don't just visualize big cars and big houses, but visualize the actions you'll take to make it happen.

Be prepared. Have everything you need readily accessible.

» Office supplies
» Digital devices
» Research tools

Anything you require to work on the current phase of your flight plan should be close at hand. When you're prepared, it prevents you from squandering your time and losing progress.

The point is to allot time *every* day—including weekends, birthdays, anniversaries, and holidays—to at least think about, plan for, and work on your dream. The more disciplined you are about the little things, the easier the big things become.

When this practice becomes tedious—as it sometimes will—consider the pain of regret if your dream were to slip away. Go back to your vision—the reason you're pursuing the dream in the first place. Remind yourself of the significance of your dream and the contribution you're making by pursuing it. This is your vision, and your commitment will be rewarded as long as you persist and play to win.

This does not have to be a painful process. There are times, however, when you'll want to put it off a day… but remember—let one day slip away, and chances are good several will slip with it.

Avoid the temptation.

When you give in, you let mediocrity win. There will be plenty of time to relax once the dream is realized.

Making The Most Of Time: The P.O.W.E.R. 5™

There is no such thing as time management. The legendary personal growth expert, Earl Nightingale, teaches that you cannot manage time, only the activities you perform in the time you have. But now that you've scheduled time, how do you make better use of it?

For starters, strive for balance. Yes, you must place priority on the attainment of your goal above all other distractions, making your dream—and the pursuit of your dream—a must. But you must also be pragmatic about the demands of life.

But how can you make better use of your time, achieve more balance, execute on your flight plan and still answer all of your ever-mounting responsibilities in life? I'd like to introduce you to a simple formula for doing just that. It's called The P.O.W.E.R. 5™, and here's how it works.

First, define your top three priorities for your year. These are three goals that, once achieved, will help define this as your best year yet. They can all be different, or they may be synergistic. The key is that they inspire you and give you something big to work toward. And they should be tied to your "why". When I do this work with clients, we hone in on the areas where they are most passionate, or have put off in the past. Often times these goals encompass different areas from financial to business to lifestyle and health, to name a few.

With your top 3 priorities identified, it's time to create a structure you can use daily to establish a rhythm for steady progress. This is the P.O.W.E.R. 5™. The idea is you do five activities every day before you put your head on the pillow at night. When done daily, these actions set the tone for your week, your month and your year.

The "P" stands for Purpose. The actions you decide for yourself each day must answer you purpose and your "why". Getting clear on this is crucial for success in life and is an absolute must for mission accomplishment.

The "O" stands for Opportunities. Make sure your actions either satisfy current opportunities or create new ones that bring you closer to the realization of your dream. They key is to stay true to your vision; almost anything can look like an opportunity, but which ones should you commit to? That can be answered with our next criteria.

The "W" stands for Win-Win-Win. This is particularly powerful for entrepreneurs, and can be used outside of business as well. When someone approaches you with an opportunity, the assumption is there is something in it for them, otherwise they wouldn't be offering it to you in the first place. The part you have to determine is if it creates a win for you as well, making for a win-win scenario. Now, take a deeper look and see if it benefits the people around you as well: your family, your friends, your clients, your employees, your community; anyone you are here to serve, particularly if they have a role in your top 3 priorities and your mission. The closer you get to a win-win-win situation, the more powerful that activity will be.

The "E" stands for Excitement. Your passion and enthusiasm will carry you a long way, much further than talent and education. This, my friend, is the jet fuel of success. Enthusiasm will dictate how high, fast and far you fly in life.

If you are having a challenge being enthusiastic about the march toward your dreams, look deeper to see how you can reframe it and find the joy in it. And if you cannot get excited about an action, find a way to outsource it. And if you cannot outsource it, find a way to get rid of it altogether.

The "R" stands for Results. You must be working toward results every day. This doesn't mean you'll see results every day, but you must discipline yourself to do result-producing activities every single day, particularly as they pertain to your top 3 priorities and your mission.

So, how do we put this to use? Let me start by sharing my personal P.O.W.E.R. 5™ and then I'll share a resource with you to really get you powered up for more productivity and focus in your day.

Each day, I accomplish activities that fall under the following categories:

» **Mindset and spirituality**: This includes gratitude exercises, some meditation, and a visualization of my goals and the actions I must take to make my dreams reality.

» **Learning and growth**: I spend an hour or more reading or researching to expand my personal and professional growth.

» **Fitness**: I push my body with weight training, core strengthening, and cardio training in the form of mountain biking or running. I strive to do each 3 days a week, alternating days in between.

» **Work my craft**: Either actively coaching, or speaking and writing keynotes and presentations.

» **Content creation**: Compile my knowledge and experience into live trainings, writings, or programs like F.L.I.G.H.T. School To Success™ and High-Altitude University™.

These are the five areas I work on every business day, and I'm as productive and energetic as I've ever been. When I accomplish actions in these five areas, I know I've put in a great day. The rest of the chaos of life can wait until these priorities are satisfied.

I've put together a complete exercise on The P.O.W.E.R. 5™, and you can access it by going to www.FlightPlanToSuccess.com/POWER5.

Work On Your Dream Every Day. Don't just plan it, *schedule* at least an hour or more every day to the pursuit of your dream. Use a calendar, cell phone alarm, whatever device you need to make it a permanent part of your life. Again, something as little as getting up an hour earlier or going to bed an hour later will help you accomplish this.

Spend Time On Your Top Commitments. These deserve your energy and focus, and will ultimately boost your efforts toward the pursuit of your goal. These areas of your life will add energy to your life—the smile of your spouse, the hug of a child, the firm grip of a friend's handshake—they all act as the ultimate performance enhancing drug. Make sure to focus time every day on:

» Family: read books, play games, laugh, spend dinner face-to-face, and share your enthusiasm for their triumphs as well as your own. The key is to *be present*.

» Health and Spiritual Well-being : start the day off with some quiet mediation and reflection; get your heart rate up and do some exercise—even 20 minutes will change your whole day.

» Career: it's easy to turn away from a career when it may not be in alignment with your purpose. Be cautious not to mentally check out until your dream is supporting your lifestyle.

» Social Life: surround yourself with people who believe in you and support your dreams. Share your joys, your frustrations, and your lessons.

Plan for these. Too many high-achievers focus the majority of their time to the pursuit of their big goals. Avoid making this mistake at all costs by enjoying life along the way. Take in the passions of your life. Take in the joys, the triumphs and the gifts of life. They will empower you to push on, and remind you why you're in the game for in the first place. Going after a big dream is amazing. It brings out the best in you and highlights your supporters as the gifts of life that they are. This is why it's a shame more people don't strive for an amazing life. The trials and challenges along the road to our dreams make the important things—family, friends, our health, and the journey itself—so much more precious.

Enjoy life. Enjoy the people in your life. Take time to appreciate and enjoy them. You'll be so glad you did.

There's No Time Like The Present

It's easy to fall into the slumber of naiveté that time is infinite—but our days in this life are numbered. Since you don't know for sure how much life you have, live like there is no guarantee of tomorrow—because there isn't.

The good news: you never have to do it alone. As you will discover, the right people, assisting you in the right areas, can be very powerful leverage of time as you build your fight plan to your true vision.

The clock is ticking. The time to pursue your dreams is now.

☑ Flight Plan Checklist

List 5 action steps you will take to gain altitude on your dreams and focus your time on your dreams.

☐ What time(s) of the day are you willing to dedicate solely to the pursuit of your vision?

☐ What do you see as your biggest consumer of time outside of work and family?

☐ What is the exact date that you will achieve your dream?

How do you plan to spend time focused on family, friends, your health and your career?

CHAPTER 5

MONEY: THE JET FUEL TO POWER YOUR MISSION

Jet fuel powers your aircraft and dictates how high, how fast, and how far you will fly. More jet fuel means more options—and managing jet fuel on any mission is one of the highest priorities of any pilot.

Most of our missions lasted several hours, sometimes as long as 10 hours in duration. With no in-flight refueling capability and often miles out at sea or over hostile territory, the option of landing for more fuel simply did not exist.

That is why it was paramount to depart on the mission with enough fuel, and to monitor the burn rate of the fuel during flight to ensure we would have plenty to accomplish the mission and arrive at our destination.

When it comes to pursuing your dreams, money is jet fuel... *financial* jet fuel.

Understanding how to tap resources to fund your dream is paramount to seeing your dreams through to the end. Whether your vision is to start a business or give to charity, if you have enough money to deploy assets and enough time to do it, you can save the mission and keep it from crashing into the ground.

What Money Is Not

I'm not a fan of negative words—don't, no, not—when it comes to making a directive statement. Too often when you introduce those words into a sentence, the receiver of the message subconsciously removes them from the context of what you said. For example, say, *don't forget to pay the mortgage* and it becomes *forget to pay the mortgage.*

I believe in asking for *exactly* want you want. Politely say, *please pay the mortgage*, and it will get done.

So with that out of the way, allow me to contradict myself.

Here's what money is NOT:

Money is not a barrier to success; money is a conduit to success.

Money is not a "hold back" to getting what you want; money is a facilitator for obtaining more freedom and flexibility.

Money is not an excuse; rather money is an answer.

Unfortunately, too many of us create excuses for why we cannot—or will not—go after our big dream. And many times they boil down to a false belief that success and fulfillment are only meant for people with lots of money.

The fact is, even high-achievers have money issues; they have mortgage and car payments, their kid's college tuition. And yes, even high-achievers over-leverage themselves sometimes.

This is not to say money may not be a concern—or that it's not important. But it should *not* be the limiting factor in pursuing your dream.

Money As An Indicator

A big shift I made a few years back was getting over the sticker shock of things I held in high regard. Whether the item was a car, a watch, or an item on a restaurant's menu, I tweaked the way my brain interpreted the price. After all, it's only a number.

Some will look at a fine automobile and gasp at the sticker price. Others will look at the price and appreciate the value of the automobile that much more.

Price point is simply an indication of the market value— but you can also look at it as the indication of how committed you must be to owning that item. Perhaps the difference between lunch at your favorite bistro and a Tiffany's diamond bracelet is the level of commitment required to have them.

When determining your level of commitment, ask yourself these questions:

Why is it priced at that level? Is it value, reputation, or both?

Is that item necessary, or can I use something else without compromising the attainment of the goal?

How can I add more value in order to elevate my own economy?

Gary Vaynerchuk, author of the book *Crush It,* is a man who made a tremendous impact on me as an entrepreneur by teaching me the power of elevating my game by adding more value to the world. And he lives his message every day.

Gary took his genuine passion for wine and transformed his family business into a multi-million dollar brand. He did not do it through private funding, angel investors, or taking out loans—all viable options to funding your dream—but rather, he did it through what he calls "sweat equity" and hustle.

He busted his ass day and night to add more value than anyone else to the marketplace . He posted on relevant blogs, paid attention to trends, and did one of the most important things to create success in business and life—he listened. He listens to his customers, he listens to other experts, and he listens to his fans.

The result is massive success and enough capital to fund just about any project he could possibly want. In short, Gary made himself more valuable by investing his time and attention into learning more and giving value.

Gary is the real deal.

Keeping Perspective On Money

It has been said time and time again that money can't buy happiness. And it's true. You can be miserable and rich, too. But the difference is that money provides more flexibility. Money gives you options—and not only better options, but more of them.

The key is to keep money in perspective. When it becomes the focus and sole purpose of your vision, that's when problems arise. When you attach too much happiness to money, that's where a hollow existence robs you of the joy and fulfillment of life.

When I went to the navy recruiter with my dream of becoming a Blue Angel, he told me I needed a college degree. I certainly didn't have the money to head straight to college, so I had to find a different way. To me, the most direct path to becoming a Naval Aviator was to join the navy—get around aviation, and earn money through the GI Bill.

While it may not have been the most entrepreneurial option, it served my purpose.

Had I strategized the many ways to get to my goal, I'm sure I would have come up with other solutions, but I wanted my dream bad. So bad, I was willing to do almost anything; and when I realized I could be around Navy Aviators—even as a mechanic—and earn money for college, I signed on the dotted line and headed for boot camp.

The point is this: never allow money to hold you back from going for your dream. And never, never, *never* make your dream solely about the money.

How Willing Are You To Risk?

Some people shudder at the thought of taking risk — anything from skydiving or launching a business. Some will avoid entering that triathlon or dating again after a painful breakup because they're afraid to risk. Afraid to fail.

It's the same with money.

We have no problem throwing in the towel early for fear of financial risk; our excuses may include:

» Been burned before—not doing it again
» Too old to recover

» Too young to get started
» Not enough experience
» Have a family to support
» Have a career to consider
» Have bills to pay/financial responsibilities
» The "Economy"

But the issue of money and time come down to priorities; is it a priority to take that chance and grow or is it a priority to remain stuck and go nowhere? Again, it's easy to understand. There are usually plenty of people within our sphere of influence to convince us our financial timidity is justified—the pursuit of *that* goal or dream is not a good idea *right now*. They may say it out of concern; they may say it because they're afraid you'll succeed and outgrow them.

I'm not talking about irresponsible risk. I'm talking about calculated risk. We take a calculated risk when we get behind the wheel of a car or when we take the controls of an airplane. There are so many factors out of our control, but rather than doing nothing, we accept a level of risk so we can reap the benefits of driving a car or traveling by plane; and our lives are ultimately better as a result of that risk.

Whether you take big risks or not, remember: money *is* available to fund your dream. Money is everywhere, so don't allow it to become an excuse that hold you back from your dream.

The average lifetime earnings of a person with a high school education is around $1.2 million (http://usgovinfo. about.com/od/moneymatters/a/edandearnings.htm). That amount goes up with each education level. While I believe education has little to do with how far a person can go in life, it's interesting to note that so many people will gawk at a million dollars when it's actually what a lot of people will make in a lifetime.

Any great endeavor involves some level of sacrifice—the question is, how much are you willing to risk to be the person you were meant to be?

Expanding your own prosperity consciousness begins to open your mind to the possibilities money can provide. It begins to dissolve the notions of loss and scarcity that come from fear-based thinking.

You owe it to yourself and the world to push your financial limits, to see how high you can raise the bar.

Avoiding Misconceptions

As odd as it may seem, some people are afraid of financial success. When faced with the very real possibility—or even concrete reality—of financial success, they freeze. They can hardly believe they've made it; and subconsciously they begin sabotaging themselves by getting rid of the money faster than they acquired it.

They tell themselves they're content to sit on the couch and live a modest lifestyle. After all, their basic needs are taken care of—they're happy. And while they may be, they're also living with a skewed perception of wealth. Perhaps t hey see jumping into an endeavor that would push them to make a million dollars, not only frightening, but selfish and greedy.

Perhaps that's how they see rich people, and they don't want to be seen the same way. Now let's look at another side of this.

Most wealthy people are more focused on health and vitality than money and greed. Most are extremely charitable—and driven to make a difference in the world.

There's nothing wrong with living a modest lifestyle. But just like placing wealth on a pedestal can be myopic, so is an unhealthy fear of prosperity.

Rather than fearing needlessly, work hard to become a person who deserves great wealth—attain it, give back, and help others do the same. Rather than wonder what it would look like, just imagine the good that can be done with an extra zero or two in your bank account.

Fuel Your Jet

Here's another interesting thing about money: it helps prevent getting scraped in life. Every person on the planet—from extremely poor to highly affluent—has problems. The wealthy often times are better at finding solutions to their problems, and it usually involves having financial resources to manage those situations.

Money:

» Brings flexibility to how, when, and where you go with your dream.
» Provides the lifestyle *you* choose —not the one society thinks you should have.
» Allows for more options—it's not the be-all-end-all.
» Serves as a catalyst—not a holdback.

Time and money have purposely been placed as the first two categories of resources you need to accomplish your dreams. This is because of how closely they're related—how one can help the other grow. Think of it this way: you have two buckets: time and money. If you're money bucket is lacking, pour in more time—if you're short on time, pour in more money.

Here is how:

If you have money to spend but are short on time, outsource the tedious tasks that rob you of time you could be focusing on your dreams. A quick internet search for "administrative assistants" or "personal assistants" could be an answer.

If you have more time than money, then invest some of that time to improve yourself and your skill sets in order to acquire more money. I'm not talking about going back to school; focus on honing skills in your natural areas of interest to turn your passions into income. There is a huge shift away from formal education and toward self-directed knowledge acquisition.

Spend time networking with like-minded achievers. These groups may not only have in their membership possible support crew members, but also people with the money and assets to help you realize your dream.

And if you're short on both time and money, tap your inner genius—the power you have always had inside you—to marshal your assets of intellect, creativity, and resilience.

Recognize money for what it is: energy.

Like any other form of energy—heat, pressure, sound, or light—money is everywhere. You just have to know how to tap into it. Once you do, you can utilize it anytime you want.

Money's abundant—it's everywhere—and you have access to all you need right now, if you simply look, listen, and ask. In the next chapter, we'll look at the category of resources that are just as abundant as money; the gear and equipment you need for you dream—assets.

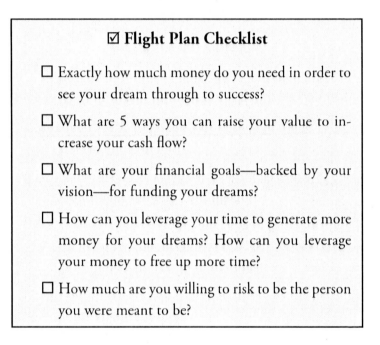

☑ **Flight Plan Checklist**

☐ Exactly how much money do you need in order to see your dream through to success?

☐ What are 5 ways you can raise your value to increase your cash flow?

☐ What are your financial goals—backed by your vision—for funding your dreams?

☐ How can you leverage your time to generate more money for your dreams? How can you leverage your money to free up more time?

☐ How much are you willing to risk to be the person you were meant to be?

CHAPTER 6

ASSETS: A CRITICAL RESOURCE FOR MISSION ACCOMPLISHMENT

The type of aircraft you fly will dictate the mission you accomplish. As a kid growing up with the dream of flight, I studied different types of aircraft and their roles in aviation. From the enormous jumbo cargo carriers capable of hauling tremendous amounts of cargo to the sleek, maneuverable fighter jets, every aircraft has its purpose.

Some are built for speed, and some are built for utility. Some aircraft can fly into the eye of a hurricane, and some can fly a wounded or sick person to medical facilities in a fraction of the time an ambulance could get them there.

Choosing the right aircraft for the mission is crucial for success.

A pilot—flying an executive from Los Angeles, California to Sydney, Australia—would opt for a luxurious Gulfstream business jet, rather than a vintage cargo plane, to get his passenger to his destination quickly and in comfort.

In the same way, you must choose the appropriate assets to accomplish your mission.

What Is Driving You?

I will never forget a cold December night that changed the path of my life forever. The kids were peacefully sleeping; the dishes from dinner were washed. My wife, Mia, was in the other room, diligently working on a marketing project.

We were struggling financially, and both of us were looking for solutions to ignite our businesses and turn our financial lives around. The difference: she was passionate about what she was doing; I was miserable.

I was miserable not so much from the financial struggle, but because I profoundly hated what I was doing. I was building a business I did not love and having zero fun in the process.

What the hell was I doing with my life?

I went from being a combat-decorated Naval Aviator to a miserable man, struggling to pay the bills with a business I loathed.

I took out a pen and a pad of paper and started writing down all the stuff I didn't have in my life—things I lacked, but thought I needed: new clothes, a new set of tires, money to pay the bills.

I was so focused on what I didn't have that I could barely breathe.

Then my email inbox chimed; there was a new message.

It was a forward from a dear friend—and in it was a video from marketing genius Eben Pagan.

The video was filmed at a live event, and Eben was presenting on the topic of marketing. He said something so powerful I literally jumped off the couch and shouted *holy shit*—much to the chagrin of my lovely wife.

Eben said, "Freedom is not *being able* to do what you want, it is about *doing* what you want."

You see, up to that point, I had been chasing a sad dream of making a ton of money to buy a ton of things, regardless of what it took. I had great determination—but a lousy motivating factor. And I was focused on *being able* to do what I wanted, versus just going out and *doing* it! I was so wrapped up in making money so I could acquire "stuff" that I was losing sight of why I got into business for in the first place.

You cannot be driven solely by the attainment of things.

Don't allow yourself to become encumbered by the illusion of needing a bunch of material stuff. If your dream is to make a ton of money—great! But learn from me and ask, first and foremost, *why*. What does it mean to you—is there more to it that fulfills you and drives you? Then set out to discover how you're going to do it.

You must know your final destination to understand what you need. Being crystal clear on what you want—and *why* you want it—is the first step in knowing what you need to make it happen.

Getting Clear On What Assets You Need

Once you have a clear goal, consider any and all resources needed to make your dream come to life. Don't hold back.

Begin by answering this question:

If money was no object, and you could get access to everything you need—what would it take to make your dream a reality?

The idea behind this drill is to get you thinking big—it also helps open up the part of your mind that is willing to accept and receive the great things in life you deserve... whether or not you think you do.

Now, list *everything*.

No doubt your list will be quite long. If your imagination is alive and well, it will probably make for a fun read later on; but for now, simply place the list in front of you.

Now, go through the list and cut it in half, keeping only the top 50 percent—this will help you focus on exactly what you really need to succeed in your journey to your ultimate vision.

At this point you may be wondering why you would pare down on assets and resources—particularly if the point was to come up with a list of crucial items, necessary for the completion of your mission.

The fact is we often take on the perilous idea that we need certain things in order to begin, let alone successfully complete something. The bigger the goal, the more stuff we think we need.

This is not only typically false, but often times serves as a cleverly disguised sabotaging technique designed to give us a way out when the going gets tough or when we are facing our greatness. By "needing" too many assets, we can easily create excuses for not succeeding—and those excuses are just another way for us to procrastinate and find a way out of doing the work necessary to succeed.

Running Lean, Keeping Your Eyes On The Target

I firmly believe the economic downturn has some unbelievably wonderful qualities. Why would I say something so outrageous? There are several reasons for this.

For one, out of turmoil and difficulty, are born some of the world's greatest innovations. Let's face it: the wheel wasn't invented out of boredom. More than likely it was invented out of a painful need to transport something really important—possibly really heavy or big—over a considerable distance.

In much the same way, out of our current economic challenges, the true champions of achievement are finding more creative and innovative ways to win. Losers are finding more and more ways to lose. Quitters are finding faster ways to give up.

Running a leaner, meaner machine is bringing new innovations in science, technology and business, as well as opening a mind spring of ideas in art, literature, human achievement, and spirituality.

People now, more than ever, are left to rely more on their imaginations and intellect—versus leaning on their checkbooks and dissolving credit—to solve problems and find solutions.

For one thing, the United States is amongst the wealthiest countries on the planet, yet we're amongst the least happy. We spend more time complaining about all the crap that clouds our lives than actually *living* our lives and being grateful for what we have. We find more ways to be miserable than any other culture on the planet. Canada and Australia are not far behind.

Some of the poorest countries on the planet, on the other hand, are home to some of the happiest people—people who find happiness and fulfillment not through things but through the development of their relationships, intellect, and enjoying experiences over material things.

Do More With Less

Believe it or not, you can accomplish a lot with what you already have in front of you. And you are capable of doing far more with far less. Could you launch your dream *right now*, with what the assets and resources you currently have?

Think critically. Use your intellect and abandon the emotional side of the thought process—drop the ego, drop the fear of scarcity, and focus on what's truly important to succeed.

What's the point? Focus.

In some cases, we make excuses for not getting started on our dream because we believe we need so many resources. Most of the time, we have more than enough resources to execute on our dream.

Another falsehood we buy into is thinking that we must have *everything* before we get started. For instance, some people will put off beginning their dream of getting in the best shape of their lives until they join a gym or buy that fancy piece of equipment they saw on TV. The fact is they could start with running through their neighborhood or getting involved in a pick-up game of basketball or some other sport just to build some momentum.

You would be surprised at what you can accomplish with what you already have. You might even be awed by your own ingenuity.

As a Naval Aviator, I attended a survival course in the Navy called SERE—Survive, Evade, Resist, and Escape. As the name implies, we were instructed on how to survive in the event our aircraft went down behind enemy lines.

In wartime, there are no hospitals, pharmacies, or grocery stores to waltz into for supplies—not when you're a downed pilot. We learned to use the environment for camouflage until we could call for help and rescue. We learned to resist capture. If that failed and we were captured, we learned how to face the challenges of life as a prisoner of war. Ultimately, the end goal was to escape and get back to safety.

SERE was as challenging a school as I have ever been through. And I learned a lot about doing more with less.

The course was set in the mountains of Maine in early May. There was still snow on the ground in parts of our training area, and highly-trained facilitators acted as our "enemy captors" whose job it was to hunt us down and interrogate us.

We did not eat for almost a week. Though trained to "live off the land", there was very little to eat...just enough to keep us going.

It was cold. It rained. Our only shelter was the makeshift hut we built to stay concealed from our determined enemy… just enough to keep the hypothermia from taking over and just enough to keep us hidden from our pursuers.

We barely slept, and when we did, it was in shifts as we watched each other's backs. We slept just enough to fight off delirium. After a while the fatigue, stress and lack of food made the entire exercise seem very real. In the end, we learned that we were far more resilient than we imagined.

Once we were captured by the enemy and detained in a very-real prisoner of war camp, the real fun began. The big takeaway for me was just how resourceful we could be; how we could perform at high levels even with a lack of resources and options. In the end, we learned that by staying focused on our mission, using our limited resources wisely, thinking outside the box, and believing in ourselves and each other, we could endure almost anything.

In SERE school, mission accomplishment was a must, even though resource availability was minimal. There is no room for excuses in situations like that, and the lessons of how resourceful and capable we really are despite little-to-no support were invaluable.

You don't have to go through SERE school to learn these lessons—but you do need to understand that you can accomplish a lot, even with a little.

Recognizing Your Assets

Knowing what you need is critical, but recognizing what you can use is just as important. From the outset, we often think we need the best or most sophisticated. Take a look back in time, and you'll find that simply isn't true...

Orville and Wilbur Wright accomplished one of the greatest feats of mankind—the first manned flight—and they did so with a very rudimentary glider. They didn't even have pilot licenses. Once the goal was achieved, they improved on the process and added a simple engine with a propeller to extend the range of the flight.

Charles Lindbergh made the first solo non-stop flight across the ocean from New York to Paris in a tiny, single engine airplane, with no front windshield, no side windows, and a cloth-covered fuselage. The flight took him over thirty-three hours. He did not wait for a jumbo jet to be invented to accomplish his vision, he used what he had available.

Chuck Yeager became the first person to break the sound barrier—in what was known as a "bullet with wings." Nobody knew for sure if an aircraft could withstand the pressures of breaking the sound barrier, yet Yeager accomplished an amazing feat with tremendous courage and the best resources he had.

The most significant accomplishments in aviation history are no different than the most significant accomplishment in your life. You have the capability of achieving something as profound as breaking the sound barrier—breaking your limitations barrier.

You simply have to know and understand the assets needed to accomplish your mission—then strap in and go full throttle toward your vision.

Keeping Inventory

Rest assured you're not limited by your initial list. None of your assets are written in stone.

As a matter of fact, you'll no doubt need to revisit your list of assets periodically. After all, some of your initial assets may have a short shelf life in the journey to your goal—a critical item needed to launch the dream, may be obsolete after the launch phase. In its place you'll need to add another asset to sustain the journey.

The key is to get going—inspired yet imperfect action is a powerful antidote for procrastinating and making excuses for not having enough resources.

As you have already learned, *you already have everything you need to accomplish anything you want.* Everything may not be right at your feet—but somewhere in your life you have the five critical items you will need to win and achieve your dream.

Ask And You Shall Receive

Too often, great people miss out on opportunities simply because they don't ask for what they need. Yet asking is often what it takes.

Whether you need money, assets, mentoring, help with planning, help with marketing, research, a second opinion, or just someone to vent to, *you have everything you need to accomplish anything you want.* But you may have to look, and you may have to ask--and ask more than a few times.

Let's say you need $10,000 to start a business, and you're lacking all or some of that money, what would you do? Quit? Give up? Probably not at first; at first you might request money from a bank, tap friends and relatives on the shoulder, or get creative with your own finances. No matter what, you have to raise the money if you don't immediately have it.

Here are a few things to consider if you're still uncomfortable asking for assistance:

First, winners and champions ask for assistance. Whether it be in the form of coaching, financial backing, or public affairs, high-achievers know they cannot do it alone so they reach out and ask for what they need. It takes true strength and courage to ask for help.

Second, believe in your dream and believe in yourself. These two things will give you the edge in finding the courage or the creativity to reach out and ask for what you want.

Third, be prepared. Have a concise description developed that will illustrate to people what you are working on. It doesn't have to be a sales pitch, and you don't have to have all the answers to every question. But the more passionately you speak about your dream, and the more prepared you are in your planning, the more apt people will be to help you out. This is why the Flight Plan To Success™ is so critical!

Fourth, be persistent. Not everyone you talk to will see your vision or buy into it. That's okay. Find the people who do, and look for more people like them.

One last thing: finding solutions to your own challenge first will go a long way in demonstrating to people why they should back you and believe in you. Persistence and imagination demonstrate a level of commitment far beyond pure passion and exuberance.

Talk about your dream often. Work on your flight plan daily. Pursue it with vigor and people *will* support you. Those people appear in your life more when you are focused on the people who support you versus those who do not. The more resolute you are in your "why", the more efficiently you'll find and attract the right people. More on that in the next chapter!

☑ Flight Plan Checklist

What are the 5 most critical assets you need to make your dream happen?

☐ How will you get those 5 assets?

☐ What is your action plan for asking for the assets you need?

☐ What improvisations can you make if certain assets are not accessible?

☐ What is the boldest action you will have to take to get the assets you require?

CHAPTER 7

PEOPLE: THE BACKBONE OF EVERY MISSION

By now, you understand the analogies of time being like altitude, and money like jet fuel. And while your assets and resources are like your airplane, one of the most critical components of any mission is a strong crew working in concert with the pilot. While Hollywood likes to portray a maverick pilot calling his own shots and standing as the lone hero at the end of the day, the truth is no pilot can succeed without a solid support crew.

I'll never forget Selection Day. Selection Day is a Naval Aviation's version of Christmas morning. This is the day the student pilot learns what type of aircraft they'll fly for the remainder of their career. For me, flying jets was a childhood dream, because it was a basic requirement to become a Blue Angel. Only tactical jet pilots are selected for the Blues, so if my dream was to come true, today was make or break. This fateful day ended with me in the top 5 of my class; I knew I had a solid shot at jets. When the selection board convened, only two jet slots were awarded, and I was selected to fly the P-3C Orion, a multi-engine turboprop aircraft designed for anti-submarine warfare. It was as far away from tactical jets as you could get, and I was devastated.

When you think fighter jets, think Ferrari. When you think P-3's, think Winnebago...on a road trip...with a slightly dysfunctional family! I was 1 of 4 pilots on a crew of 12 people with academic backgrounds ranging from MBAs to GEDs. Some of my enlisted crew members were older than me. Hell, the aircraft was older than me!

But while I was extremely disappointed to miss out on the dream of flying jets, I quickly learned how valuable each and every crew member was. My radar operator, for instance, was amazing at finding targets and isolating them for us to track and monitor. If the radar malfunctioned, which it sometimes did, my radar operator could troubleshoot and repair it within minutes. Even as a highly-trained aviator, I couldn't do that.

My crew taught me just how important having a highly-skilled team of dedicated professionals with me could be. There is no way I could have accomplished a single mission without those amazing men and women. And I'm deeply grateful for every one of my crew members, as each one contributed to my success, both personally and professionally.

Whether on a training flight or a complex combat mission, every pilot needs the backing and support of tremendous professionals with years of experience and knowledge to help them succeed.

Every day, worldwide, tens of thousands of missions rely on this level of teamwork to ensure the success of each flight. Yet most people underestimate the importance of having a solid team in place for planning and executing the mission of achieving their goals.

Connecting to the right people can set your flight plan into mach speed. Learn the strategies for identifying, selecting, and building a strong support crew now. Doing this will enable you to maximize your efforts by leveraging the talents of the excellent people you bring aboard your mission.

Anything Can Happen With The Right People in Place

Flying into the dark skies of uncertainty is always easier with an experienced flight crew onboard.

Pursuing your dream is no different.

Sadly, too many people take the "Lone Ranger" approach to achievement and assume they have to go it alone. Taking personal responsibility for your own success is paramount, but seeking the counsel of trusted advisors is critical for getting to your ultimate destination.

Time, money, assets—all three can be attained quickly if all the pieces fall perfectly into place. But what if time is limited, or what if you lack the money to finance your dream? What if you require a major asset and have no immediate means of acquiring it?

The answer, of course, is perhaps the single most critical piece of the puzzle: connecting with the right people. With a solid team in place, you can accomplish *anything*.

Here's why a strong support crew is so important:

» **Prior experience.** Different people bring a variety of experience levels to the table; when they are willing to share what they've learned, it can be invaluable for your future success. Someone who's been down the road before can shed light on how to accomplish the mission and perhaps avoid the pitfalls of success, etc.

» **Different perspectives.** Outsiders may "see the forest for the trees" better than you—not because they're better or smarter than you, but because they are not directly involved in the process, and therefore, less emotionally invested.

» **The power of influence.** One person—with the right connections, with access to resources, and a desire to help find the solutions—can make the difference between coming up short and landing safely at your destination.

» **The home-field advantage.** A fanbase not only encourages you to get started—they pick you up when you fall, help you stay motivated when you get tired, and remind you of what you are doing it all for in the first place. These are not "yes" people, but the kind of people who keep you grounded and help keep the big picture in view.

But you have to be careful. Not everyone will qualify for your team. Strive to align with people who are committed to the same values, ethics, and focus as you. Look to work with those who are operating at the top of their game, and if possible, at a higher level than you. Be sure the people with whom you align are a solid fit for your dream, and you for theirs. You may have to sift through a long list of people to find your team, but once you do, few things can stop you on your rise to the top.

How To Build A Support Crew

Who you select as your support crew is as important as making the decision to go after your dream in the first place. Just reaching out to friends or family is great, but it may not be enough.

Here's the interesting thing about people: we have an innate desire to learn and to matter. Our desire to learn is fed by all of our senses. We love to hear other people talk about their lives and all the things they find interesting. And our desire to matter is what causes us to want to give advice when someone complains to us about an ailment, frustration, or the pain-in-the-ass people we often run into in life.

Start by getting crystal clear on the type of people you need on your crew to accomplish the mission. As a Naval Aviator I flew with lots of different people; and I can tell you, I did not always get along wonderfully with all of them. At least not at first. I flew with good buddies, but our friendship on the ground did not translate to us being the most effective crew in the air. I also flew with people I did not see eye-to-eye with on the ground, but once airborne, we were a force to be reckoned with.

Success breeds success. If you have a successful relationship with someone, they may be great crew members—or they may not. And people that you know who are very skilled and knowledgeable, but hard to connect with normally, may just end up becoming excellent allies on your path to success.

Evaluate your potential support crew and critically assess the following:

» Are they competent in the field you are delving into? A competent personal trainer may be your best resource for a fitness goal, but may not be the best person to help you with the legal side of launching a business.

» Can you trust them? Just because they are knowledgeable doesn't necessarily mean they will have your best interest in mind.

» Will they be brutally honest with you at all times? Sometimes old friends have a tendency to sugar-coat the truth. Going with a straightforward person may save you time, money, frustration—even your life.

» Will they appreciate you and your dream? Avoid people who scoff, judge, or belittle you and your dreams at all costs. These people do not always mean harm, but they are dream killers and shall not be tolerated.

» Are they winners and high-achievers? Endeavor to surround yourself with the best people you can, in everything you do—particularly in the area of achieving your goal. Seek the advice of successful, optimistic people. These are the ones who will help you find a way when all you initially see are obstacles.

Sometimes you'll run across the one person who holds the key to achieving your goal—or he'll know the person with the key. Sometimes, your enthusiasm alone stirs a memory of a resource they came across that can fulfill your desire.

Talking about your dream has a way of pulling contacts and resources seemingly out of thin air.

Sharing your dream opens doors to:

» Partnerships
» Sponsorships

» Joint ventures
» Fundraising
» Sound advice
» Inspiration

When we share our dreams and goals with the world, we awaken the world around us. Don't hide your dream—never hide your dream . Because here's the secret: the more you share your dream, the more you breathe life into it. Share it with as many people as possible, and sooner or later, you will find the key people to help you achieve it. It is a core tenet of leadership to convey and share your vision. Do this, and the right people will appear.

Imagine talking passionately about your dream, only to spark the imagination of someone who offers a solution to achieving your goal. Then imagine that same person, being so inspired by your drive to achieve, that they share your story with a friend, a spouse, a colleague, or a child who, in turn, is inspired to set out on the path to achieving their own big dream. That is a powerful gift you give to the world simply by showing up to your dream.

Flying First-Class With High-Altitude People

Often times you'll encounter a high-level person such as an industry leader, top executive, coach, or renowned personality who may be a perfect fit for your support crew. These high-level people can be an excellent resource for learning how to achieve success, particularly if they have excelled in a field you are aspiring to succeed in yourself.

In these cases, we may see people who are a little ahead of us on the journey to success and think they are out of reach for us, but that may just be insecurity rearing its ugly head. Instead, think of how you can build a relationship with them. Where and how can you add value to them? What talents and experience do you have that can contribute to an area they are most excited about?

In order to answer these questions, learn as much as you can about these people, and, if practical, spend some time with them. Before reaching out to them, invest some time "gathering intelligence":

» Check out their websites
» Read their blogs
» If they are published authors, read their books
» Watch their presentations and videos
» And, most importantly, reach out to them

Through learning more about them, and what's important to them, you can find ways to add value to their lives.

Taking a successful person to lunch can pay big dividends in the knowledge and insight you'll gain from having a conversation with someone who has achieved high levels of success.

Having the valuable information and wisdom of key individuals who have gone before us can make the difference between a smooth flight and a thrill ride.

Feeling Worthy Of Support

One of the toughest obstacles to overcome in enlisting a support crew is the feeling of worthiness—and fear of rejection. Your vision means everything to you, and the thought of a high-value person declining to participate in your dream may be frightening.

You may think of the ideal person to support or advise you—but suddenly, you fear they either don't know you or don't think highly enough of you to take a chance on your vision. Maybe you don't feel confident enough in your dream to ask for assistance in achieving it. Maybe you don't believe enough in yourself to follow through and see the mission to the end.

It is imperative to rise above those thoughts and honor yourself and your dream. You are more capable than you imagine, so get on board with the idea that you can and *will* accomplish the mission. Your mission is only going to be successful if *you* are at the helm. The fact that you're piloting the mission illustrates your value, and your value is what any person will want to invest in.

What if you have great people you can reach out to, but you are afraid to ask for help? What if more than rejection, you are intimidated by the notion of looking needy, incompetent, or ridiculous?

Most successful people are more than willing to lend a hand. It's a sign of excellence! And when you've exhausted all avenues searching for the solution on your own, it can sometimes be that one phone call you make to a coach, mentor or friend that makes all the difference in your life.

One of the things I love most about the work I do is watching as my clients make that right-angle turn and get back on track to their dreams after working through a challenge together. Truthfully, I learn a great deal from these meetings, too, so know that by reaching out and asking for help, you not only get tremendous advice from people who have gone before you, but you just may inspire in them a new sense of energy and excitement. It's the synergistic exchange of ideas and energy that makes connecting with excellent people so powerful.

Getting others on board with your dream is easier than you may imagine. If you detach yourself from the acceptance of others, and focus on the meaning and purpose of the end goal, you will constantly meet like-minded people who just may be tremendous partners in your success.

If you find yourself constantly desiring acceptance from others, it is time to refocus that energy on you; your own acceptance of *yourself*. You are good enough, "as-is". You are awesome as you are. Just get busy making your dreams your reality, and the right people will show up.

Finding The Diamonds In The Rough

Sometimes we intentionally find members of our support crew—and sometimes they find us.

Have you have ever run into a person you haven't seen in awhile, and experienced the thrill of seeing them again? If so, you're familiar with the magical feeling of synergy. The ironic part is that these "chance" run-ins happen more often than most people realize. And more often than not, they happen for a reason bigger than we can imagine.

Likewise, there are times when it's difficult to recognize a person who could become a valuable member of your team; we may be overlooking the diamonds in the rough.

One caveat about speaking often and freely about your dream is that you will attract interest from all kinds of people—including some you may not initially think will be beneficial to your endeavor.

Do yourself a favor and slow down the judgment process; perhaps suspend it altogether.

If you remain open-minded, people will surprise and even amaze you with what they can do. A solution to your dream may come from a person who works for you, a relative you don't think highly of, or even a child. If you close your mind to certain possibilities, there is no way they *all* can be realized.

One of the most brilliant people I have ever come across is a man by the name of Seth Godin. I've learned a lot from Seth, and one of my favorite lessons came from a speech he gave where he talked about differentiating yourself in the marketplace.

During the presentation, Godin described the invisibility of cows; how we drive by a cow and never even notice it because they are so commonplace. "But if the cow was *purple*," suggests Godin, "you'd notice it!" That purple cow is remarkable.

Just like those cows, the people we need are all around us. But if we don't provide the platform for them to be remarkable in our lives, we won't notice them. However, by engaging them, asking questions and *listening*, we get to know them, not from a place of our agenda, but from authentic curiosity. And when we give the people in our vicinity the means by which to become "purple cows" and stand out by providing solutions to our needs, we open the door to allowing their true excellence to shine. We collaborate. We elevate each other. We fly formation. Then, we all become remarkable.

Leading The Team, Leading The Mission

Now that you have begun to build a team, it's time to lead them. As proud as I am of the missions I flew and the aircraft I piloted, nothing compares to the experience of leading amazing men and women in demanding operations and conditions.

There are differing opinions on leadership; some believe leadership is innate—that leaders are born—and some believe it is learned and developed. I'm in the second group. I believe anyone can be an effective leader if they put their focus into understanding leadership.

Leadership isn't defined by a title. Leadership is not about experience, reputation, income, pedigree, position, or the volume of one's voice. Leadership is about heart. Leadership is about vision; the ability to create a picture of the future and believe in it, then see it through to the end. Leadership is about communication.

Leadership is also about compassion. And that compassion comes from the leader being more than just casually interested in their team, but absolutely committed to their success. The part of leadership that is sometimes frightening is the requirement for the leader to be vulnerable at times; to admit doubts and fears—if not to others, than at least to themselves.

In order for you to bring an amazing team together and get them to fly formation to the finish line, it is imperative that you understand your people. Get to know them deeper than their roles. Know what drives them; what their passions are. What their vision is. What their "why" is, and if necessary, help them find it for themselves.

For your team to operate at their peak potential, each member has to feel they are a part of something bigger than just the goals and checkpoints on the flight plan. They must feel they are part of something bigger than themselves, bigger than you. And they have to feel appreciated and valued.

The role of a leader demands that they emit compassion every step of the way, even when the chips are down. One of the most important lessons I learned by working my way up through the ranks from enlisted aircraft mechanic to combat-decorated Naval Aviator was the phrase, "Praise in public, criticize in private." What this axiom demands of the leader is a level of maturity and self-control to know when to praise and when to criticize, and to do so appropriately. You have likely experienced episodes where a person in a leadership position lambasted a subordinate, or used fear to run the show. In some cases, that behavior works. However, if you want to be a High-Altitude Leader, and accomplish great things with extraordinary people, there is no room for self-indulgent tirades and tantrums.

So how do we stay in our power and maintain an even keel? How do we place our team members in roles that will set them up for success and ensure mission accomplishment? How do we lead *ourselves* and set the example of excellence?

It starts with self-respect; seeing our own value and trusting ourselves to do our best always. It means erasing the idea of being perfect, and instead be excellent; excellence comes from honoring ourselves for who we are instead of our title or accomplishments or failures or missteps. When we come from a place of self-respect and commitment to our highest values, we extend that example out to all the people with whom we come in contact. We inspire them to be their best and to rise to new levels of excellence.

That is true leadership. That is true influence.

Summing Up Your Support Crew

Your support team will be the most valuable asset you have, and the quality of your leadership will determine how effective that team will be. Be committed to your team, and your team will be committed to you. Be passionate and focused, and the right people will follow. Be true to yourself and your vision, and you will inspire incredible people to do remarkable things. Together.

☑ Flight Plan Checklist

☐ Who are your five support crew members?

☐ What qualities do they possess that inspired you to choose them?

☐ How and when will you approach each of them?

☐ What is your strategy for accessing their talents and coordinating their efforts in your pursuit?

☐ How will you thank them or reward them when the mission is accomplished?

CHAPTER 8

PILOTING YOUR VISION

A mission hinges on many factors, but there is one in particular that ultimately determines the success or failure of that mission: the pilot.

The success of any flight depends on the pilot utilizing his resources—altitude, fuel, aircraft, and support crew—and applying his skill, knowledge, and focus to the mission at hand.

When it comes to your missions in life, you are the pilot of your vision.

Now that you understand your resources—time, money, assets, and people—you need to know how to apply this knowledge to the proper execution of your flight plan.

It's time to address the adjustments necessary to utilize the information we've discussed to this point. It's time to develop you into the best pilot—the pilot of your vision—you can be.

It's time for a little flight school.

Ground School

When I walked into the classroom for the first time, I couldn't believe my eyes. It was an oppressively muggy day in Pensacola, and I was running on about three hours of sleep—I was so excited for that day.

It was my long-awaited dream, the day I dreamt about since I was a kid. The day I had worked so hard for. The one I had pictured in my mind for years.

This was the day I was told would never come. I was finally in flight school.

Within minutes of the first class starting, I was slapped in the face with the cold hand of reality. A work load of studying, test-taking, reading, more studying, and more testing met me head on for the next several weeks.

I watched as dozens of my classmates got dropped from the program. We hadn't even set foot in an airplane before two of my best buddies had their dreams of becoming Naval Aviators dashed forever. By the time I would graduate, almost 80% of my original class would wash out and go on to do other things in the Navy.

Only after I had passed everything—all the physical exams, near-drowning incidents in the water survival pools, academic challenges, and late night study sessions—did I finally strap into the pilot's seat.

That's flight school.

When I finally stood front and center in the assembly hall on September 7, 2001 and had my coveted Navy Wings of Gold pinned to my chest, I could barely keep it together. All those years of dreaming, believing, sacrificing, and persisting had come to this. All the rejections, all the doubts, all the tears, they all led me to this day. I looked down at my chest and saw the gold wings. It almost seemed like make-believe; like I was wearing a costume on Halloween. But this was real. I had done it. It was the childhood dream I had chased so doggedly for so long.

And now it was time to fly.

Flight school was tough, but only because the dream on the other end of it was so significant. It was proof that dreams come true, as long as the dreamer evolves into the doer.

Dreamers have been called movers of mountains, creators of solutions, birth-givers of ideas—even heroes.

But you have to admit, the doers—those who take the action necessary to make the dream a reality—are the true champions. After all, it's one thing to say you're going to do something, and something completely different to go out and do it.

It is a true gift to know your mission in life with absolute certainty. It is a gift you deserve to give yourself, and in order to give it, you must connect to your purpose and passion.

Then it's a matter of taking action—*purposeful* action—toward the accomplishment of your vision. It's a decision to act on your true passions, to answer the urge that lies in every single one of us to go for something significant.

It's not enough to do something just for the sake of doing it, or to half-ass your way through the pursuit of your dream for the sake of saying you're going after it.

It's the focused effort, unbridled enthusiasm, and dogged determination that will see you through.

The First Rule Of Flight School: Understand Your Capabilities

In order to accomplish any mission, the pilot must go into it believing he will succeed. Taking inventory of the aircraft, the fuel, the support of the crew, and having a belief in his natural abilities is crucial to getting the aircraft off the ground.

As the pilot of your vision, your mission starts with a healthy belief in your dream—and in your ability to make it a reality. I can assure you, every student pilot starts with basic fundamentals before they ever set foot in the cockpit, but it is the belief in oneself that ultimately matters the most.

Some of the training in aviation fundamentals is tedious. Learning things from the basic structural components of the aircraft to the science behind weather can be boring to an enthusiastic student pilot who only wants to fly at the speed of sound in a sleek fighter jet.

But just as a pilot must understand how their aircraft operates, you must understand how *you* operate. While it's important to be aware of the limitations of the aircraft, pilots are more interested in the aircraft's capabilities.

When I went through flight school in 2000 to 2001, I was trained in the Beechcraft T-34C *Mentor*. Aptly named, the *Mentor* is an excellent aircraft for student pilots to cut their teeth on. It has enough power to get a student out of trouble should they put the aircraft in a stall or slow-flight situation. It has the perfect blend of maneuverability and stability to allow the pilot to learn complex flight regimes without sudden loss of control. And, it's a whole lot of fun to fly!

That said, the first time I laid eyes on the *Mentor*, I thought it looked like a toy. To me, it looked like a vintage war plane from the Second World War—one that might snap in half in a strong cross wind or hard landing. But once I flew the aircraft, I developed a healthy respect for just how sturdy it really was.

When I advanced to the aerobatics phase of flight training—flights that incorporate loops, rolls, and maneuvers that place a decent amount of G-force, or G's, on pilot and airplane—I really began to respect the *Mentor*.

You see, I was more interested in what the airplane could *do*. At first I was concerned about its limitations—then I learned to push the aircraft to the edges of its *capabilities*.

I was willing to fly the aircraft over water, pulling G's and flying it hard because I had the experience of seeing what it could do in capable hands.

Is it possible to push the *Mentor* past its limits and damage or crash it as a result? Absolutely. But if you understand the aircraft's capabilities, you can maximize those values to the greatest extent possible.

You must do the same inventory on yourself. At first glance, you may think you're not capable of handling the high-G demands of your big dream of success. In reality, you're *more* than capable.

And just as it's possible to out-fly the capabilities of a T-34, it's possible for you to "out-fly" your own capabilities. The key is being in-tune with what you *can* do and gradually pushing your comfort zone to accomplish more than you originally thought possible.

To do this, take a quick self-assessment. Set a timer for thirty minutes and write all you've accomplished to date. Think of it as your aerobatic flight test. After all, success rarely comes from flying straight and level. Success comes from flying those high-G loops and barrel rolls of life—and you've flown more than you may realize.

Write down anything that even remotely feels like an accomplishment.

Begin by considering what you've done in the areas of:
» Family
» Friends
» Your community
» Business
» Sports
» Arts
» Spirituality

Note anything you've accomplished in these areas—and the impact you made in the process. Focus on the facts; try not to pass judgement on the scope or impact of your accomplishment.

Example:

» Third grade, sang solo in the school play—everyone cheered.
» High school, ran for student body treasurer—won with dignity.

» Played on the school football (or any other) team. Even if you sat on the bench, you succeeded. Even if you tried out for the team and didn't make it, you succeeded as long as you never quit.

» Volunteered at a shelter for battered women.

» Read to the local kindergarten class.

» Coached little league.

» Started a business.

» Got married.

» Became a parent, committed to being my best everyday.

As you can see, you don't have to win a Super Bowl or invent a light bulb to be awesome—you don't even have to be publicly recognized or adored to be a winner.

Debriefing Each Mission

After each mission—from routine training flights, to long haul transport lifts—pilots take time to debrief themselves and their crew on what they learned.

Taking time to assess what went well, and what can be improved, is addressed on the spot so adjustments can be made before the next mission. This is crucial for growth and improvement...and is standard operating procedure in Naval Aviation.

You don't have to wait until the end of your journey to do the same assessment of your mission. Do it at the end of every phase of your mission. Do it at the end of every day, week, month, year.

I discuss this in depth in my course, F.L.I.G.H.T. School To Success™, and this brief description will give you a good start on tracking and debriefing your way to your overall mission.

Making your list of accomplishments is your first example of debriefing. What did you learn about yourself by listing your successes and triumphs?

This exercise is crucial to your future success. When you write down all your accomplishments and positive achievements, you focus on your capabilities the way a pilot focuses on the capabilities of their aircraft. You have proof—*facts*—to contradict the biggest lie most people tell themselves: *I suck ... I don't deserve this ... I'll never accomplish this ... I've never won anything in my life.*

If you tried and failed but didn't give up, you won. If you gave yourself to a cause bigger than your own, you have won. If you helped someone else win, you won.

Too often, we get wrapped up in what we've done wrong, or what we've failed to do. We're quick to remember how many times, and the many different ways, we've failed.

It's time to stop seeing our "failures" in a negative light. It's better to applaud our efforts, and focus on the lessons learned, then apply those lessons to improve future performance.

In doing so we'll find confidence in knowing that, despite our human tendencies to falter from time to time, we remain capable. We accomplish amazing things and have tremendous impact on the world, whether we notice it or not.

The next step is to look for patterns in your achievement. In flight school, it's easy to get discouraged when things get tough—and they do. With an 80 percent attrition rate, it sometimes feels as if tying your flight boots incorrectly will get you dropped from the program.

To keep self-doubt at bay, learn to account for patterns of successful behavior and thought processes that run through your various achievements.

These are typically character traits. Things like how well you respond to pressure, how you handle adversity and defeat. These are common traits of excellence, and important tenets to possess in your everyday life.

Flying Into A Headwind

In aviation, one of the many things pilots must keep a vigilant eye on is the amount of fuel they have—and, in particular, the fuel burn rate.

Fuel burn rate equals the amount of fuel burned per hour of flight time. Pilots calculate this rate at different points throughout the flight to ensure they will have plenty of fuel to not only arrive at their destination, but to safely divert, or fly to an alternate airport in the event of inclement conditions.

The same discipline is necessary in the achievement of your ultimate vision. In aviation, if you run out of fuel, you might end up crashing or ditching the aircraft. In life, if you're not constantly keeping track of your mental, emotional and financial burn rate, you risk burning out before realizing your dream.

Being "stuck" is analogous to flying into a fierce headwind in an aircraft. It doesn't take long for a robust headwind to sap your fuel and put you at risk of fuel starvation. So how do you handle a headwind? The answer: descend or climb to a different altitude where the winds are less severe. Coming up short of the destination or aborting the mission is not an option in Naval Aviation.

And settling for less than you deserve or aborting the pursuit of your dream is not an option for you, either.

So, if you are debating as to whether or not you should pursue your true mission in life, if you are feeling exhausted by life or thinking now may not be the best time to go after your dreams, let's figure out how you can decrease the headwinds in your life and ensure you don't run out of fuel before you get to your destination.

To start, take a few minutes for another self-assessment. This time take note of the things you do on a daily basis that suck the life right out of you.

This list may include:

» Your job
» People
» Too many commitments

These things are the headwind you are flying against—the success of your mission depends on you finding a way out of that headwind:

» Reframe the context of the situation; or
» Eliminate your headwind.

Example:

You hate mowing the lawn; you have two options:

Reframe how you think about it. Instead of focusing on yard work, think of it as taking pride in your home. Consider the health benefits of the physical exertion. Enjoy the compliments you get from friends, family, and neighbors. If nobody's giving you compliments, give them to yourself. Nobody will see the value in your hard work if you don't see it first.

Eliminate the headwind. Pay someone else to do the mowing for you.

Make your flight path to your dream easier by first recognizing the things that drag you down and eliminating them altogether. If elimination is not an option, then think critically about how you can reframe the situation to better fit your needs.

Sometimes simply recognizing the benefits and values of the situation can add new life because your focus is now on the benefits, the drudgery and pain.

Spin Recovery

Sometimes you can be fired up about life, totally going for it, when a sudden and unexpected setback knocks you on your butt. It happens. The key is to not allow these setbacks to put you into a tailspin.

As a Naval Aviator, I had a flight manual as thick as a phonebook that included detailed instructions on how to handle in-flight emergencies. We were required to know those procedures cold—breaking out a fifteen pound instruction manual in the middle of an engine fire is not the best way to avert catastrophe.

So we studied, committed to memory, and trained on these critical procedures—including spin recovery.

In a spin, the aircraft departs controlled flight—the pilot suddenly loses control of the airplane. When this occurs, the nose of the airplane drops, the aircraft begins a violent rotation toward the earth, and the pilot begins a corkscrewing thrill ride straight down.

An untrained person would probably panic. Hell, I nearly panicked the first time I was introduced to this procedure. Even a seasoned aviator, if caught off guard, will freeze for a moment at the abject terror that a sudden spin can bring about.

Entering a spin in an airplane is not much different than entering a tailspin in life. You might be pushing really hard in your career, or toward your true vision, when suddenly you find yourself spinning out of control.

Your position is downsized, your business takes a monstrous hit, you or someone you love becomes ill, or you suddenly lose passion for what you're doing with your life.

Spins happen to everyone from time to time. But those who bounce back quickly are the ones who have a spin recovery procedure in place. Here is something I teach in my program High-Altitude University™, a course named "Spin Recovery":

Step I: Pull back the throttles. If you're going full-speed in life and things suddenly get out of control, pull back. Take a break. Sometimes just stepping back from the situation will stabilize everything.

Step II: Neutralize the controls. All too often, especially when really going after something huge, there's a tendency to force things. Instead of forcing the issue, return things to neutral. If you're experiencing turmoil in your business, career or relationships, instead of trying to impose your will, let other people in your life have their say. Listen. Learn. Take it all in.

Step III: Apply rudder in the opposite direction of the spin. Once you have a sense of what the real issues are, shift your practices in a manner that allows you to make gentle yet deliberate corrections to the situation. You don't have to make a full recovery right away. Be patient with yourself here.

Step IV: Pull out of the dive. When the tumbling and spinning has stopped, cooler heads prevail, and now you can begin pulling out of the dive. Smoothly getting back to the altitude you were before all hell broke loose may take time. If you attempt to pull the nose up and climb back to your altitude before you have taken care of the chaos, it will only result in a tighter, more catastrophic spin.

Step V: Push throttles up. Once you've stabilized the situation, gotten back on altitude, and have regained a normal speed, get back in the saddle. Push the throttles up and resume flying toward your destination.

For the full program on this procedure, visit
www.HighAltitudeU.com.

The secret is to release the illusion of control first. As difficult as surrender can be for us high-achievers, a great deal of peace comes from sometimes letting go and allowing the answers to come to us, rather than us constantly trying to hunt the answers down.

Recognizing Fear And Flying Beyond It

Most pilots will not openly admit when fear is riding on their laps—but every pilot experiences it from time to time.

One of the biggest killers of the human spirit is fear. Fear is an interesting paradox; we have it installed in our DNA to keep us from doing dumb things like jumping into fire and running into traffic. Fear reminds us that it hurts to touch a hot stove. Fear alerts us when a dangerous situation is present-ing itself, and when we are unable to back away from those dangerous situations. Fear augments our performance centers of the brain/body connection and provides us with seemingly super-human capabilities.

But while fear is installed to protect us from the cruel world around us, it also responds to *perceived* danger.

And sometimes this fear is irrational.

Fear of public speaking, for instance, can stem from a per-ception of pain: the very thought of the audience laughing at you, rejecting your message, or booing you off the stage causes your brain to jump into protection mode, just as it was programmed to do from the time our early ancestors were running from saber-toothed tigers.

Fear is in our biology, and there is no way to avoid it. But we can use fear to perform better if we understand how it works. We can use it as a lever to catapult us to the next level. If we think of fear as a wave in the ocean, we can think of ourselves as surfers; we can paddle against it, we can allow the wave to wash over us, or we can sit back and allow the wave to pass us by. But if we want to achieve anything of significance in life, we have to drop in and ride the wave.

To paddle against it is like trying to conquer our fear: it becomes exhausting and counterproductive. People try to conquer fear when they believe they can make it go away per-manently. They do the thing that scares them over and over again, and get discouraged when the fear doesn't disappear. The mistake is thinking it will go away.

To allow the wave to wash over us is to allow fear to con-quer us; to be so consumed with it that it drowns us and pre-vents us from growing and moving forward.

To allow the wave to pass us by is to pretend fear isn't holding us back; to delude ourselves into playing it safe and living a mediocre life of resignation.

But to ride the wave—to surf it boldly—is to use fear as a performance-enhancing drug. It means we go after our dreams and stay one step ahead of fear. When we respect the fear, knowing when it is present, we can use it as leverage to help us perform better each time we play the game. Respecting ourselves enough to acknowledge fear, rather than deluding ourselves into thinking we're impervious to it helps us stay slightly ahead of the fear and allow it to push us forward. This is how we can use fear to push us past comfort and toward excellence.

So how do you see your fear before taking off on your mission?

First understand that fear hides itself in many costumes: procrastination, guilt, pain, anger, jealousy, judgment, indifference—just to name a few. If you find yourself making excuses for not taking action on an important project, it is often times rooted in fear.

Neglect of your health, financial struggles, and soured relationships almost always have an underlying cause stemming from fear. Fear isn't the *only* cause, mind you, but it's often a main cause.

So if you're struggling with getting started on your big vision, look inside and see where fear may be at work. Really give yourself the attention you deserve to get down to the root of the procrastination. The only requirement here is to be honest with yourself.

When I do this work with clients, we uncover some pretty deep-seated stuff. One client—we'll call him Paul—had lost several million dollars through various investments and business ventures, and was in a place of stagnation in business and life. Fear was holding him back from going after his passions, and he doubted himself when it came to running a business.

Paul had also been carrying the pain of his father's disapproval with him his entire life, and with the passing of his father several years prior, had nowhere to discharge the guilt and anguish. Instead, he attached his status and failures to his identity, and that was a root cause of his procrastination. Paul was scared to launch for fear of failing again, and solidifying his image as a financial failure.

Paul and I started by decoupling his financial status and past failures from his image he had of himself. Paul, like all of us, is not his successes nor his failures, and once he saw his own excellence and worth, his failures became a strength; they became wisdom and power instead of a badge of guilt and shame.

Paul also did something extremely courageous; he forgave his father and *himself.* He forgave his deceased father, because Paul realized his father did the best he could as a parent. No parent is perfect, and dwelling on the pain of the past doesn't serve us if we intend to move forward. But Paul's biggest victory was forgiving himself for the choices he made, the actions he took, and the results that came from both. That was the turning point for Paul. Today, he is happy, healthy, and on his way to building a lucrative business that he truly loves.

Until you find the root of your fear that fear will always be the mountain standing in the way of your destination.

But when you recognize the source of the fear, you can navigate around it.

We all encounter fear in life. But fear should not turn you back from your true vision. If you cannot navigate around the source of your fear, ride fear like a wave.

Yes, you will hit bumps along the way. You may even feel doubts about whether or not you can or should continue. These are the times when you are being tested the most; being challenged with "How bad do you want it?" But press on. Stay the course, and adjust your course as necessary.

And remember Paul's journey; when we accept ourselves for who we are, and recognize that we are not our successes, failures, status, or material "stuff", we can live with freedom and optimism.

The Most Important Sale You'll Ever Make

Pilots must make the most critical sale of all: buying into their own vision, and buying into themselves.

If a pilot lacks confidence in his ability to carry out the mission, his crew will not follow him. But if that pilot takes full responsibility for the execution of the mission—and believes without a doubt he will succeed—then he will turn doubters into believers, and skeptics into followers.

Until you buy into yourself, nobody else will.

You are the pilot of your dream—nobody else can fly the mission for you. You have the role and responsibility to carry out your life mission and achieve your ultimate vision. Believe you deserve every success you desire, and back it up with strong purpose and focused execution. You've already accomplished great things. Now it's time to step it up and go for your vision.

And don't rely on others to motivate you; motivation comes from within. Sure, a great teacher, an inspiring passage or speech, a moment that sparks your imagination can all awaken your internal motivation—your internal genius—but in the end, you are the one who dictates how high, fast, far you will go.

Believe you can outlast any headwind and change altitude as necessary to reach your ultimate destination. Take confidence in knowing you have the strategy in place to recover from the tailspins. And arm yourself with courage and poise to face your fear—admit it exists, and work on making yourself stronger, so you can push around it to realize your dream.

This isn't some hocus-pocus fairytale. This is the real formula for success.

The secret to success is you. Get comfortable with it—then strap in and get ready for the journey of your life.

☑ Flight Plan Checklist

Make a list of your successes. What are the common themes of those successes and what do they say about your character and your ability to succeed?

☐ What are some ways you can more efficiently decrease the headwinds in your life, so you have more energy to pursue your passions?

☐ What are some of the fear-based thoughts and habits that have been holding you back? How will you eliminate them from your life?

☐ Think back on a setback that was difficult to get past. What are some ways you could have flown over around or through it more effectively? How will you apply that lesson to your future challenges?

Are you truly ready to build your flight plan and fly your ultimate mission—the mission of your true vision of your life? Are you sold on the idea of your dream? How do you intend to stay focused on your vision?

CHAPTER 9

CLEARED FOR TAKEOFF

Flying is an amazing experience. The freedom of climbing above the world and gaining a new perspective is amazing. The challenge of performing complex maneuvers, managing several tasks at once, and doing so with confidence and precision is something that, once you've tasted it, will beckon you for the rest of your days.

Flight school itself is a challenge, and sometimes downright daunting. Military flight school is extremely demanding, and the standards that flight students are held to are extremely high, but with good reason. The demands of the profession require pilots to be mentally and physically strong; the rigors of flight school require tremendous focus and determination of the student pilot.

But in the end, the crucible makes the reward of earning your wings well worth the challenges and sacrifice.

You may have experienced this in your pursuit of success. In the previous chapter you listed many of your victories, and took note of how you endured and persevered along the path you took to get to those victories. You have earned your wings in life. Now it's time to set your sights on our ultimate mission: the pursuit of your greatest dream and true vision.

The time has come to fly your flight plan.

Now that you have the background on what you need to achieve your dreams and why you need to achieve them, it's time to execute your plan and get your vision off the ground.

Setting Your Destination

As a pilot, our missions are defined not just by what we accomplish, but when and where we do it. Without a clear understanding of the destination, a mission can go nowhere.

For combat missions, we had precise latitude and longitude coordinates that defined our target—and a specified time to arrive, down to the exact second.

Once we knew where we were going and when we needed to be there, the real planning could take place: how much fuel to carry, what weapons and equipment were needed, personnel required for the mission, and route of flight.

With success, and particularly the pursuit of your ultimate vision, you must be very specific and unrelenting in defining what you intend to achieve. "I want to get in shape"... or "I want to be rich" won't cut it anymore than a pilot saying "we're going flying and we'll be back later".

First, define your dream and why you're building your flight plan around achieving it. Remember your GPS—goals, purpose, strategy. Your goal is more than a destination, it's a commitment. Your dream can only be realized after you assign the purpose to it—and take meticulous accounting of where you are today.

When assessing your starting point, consider the following:

> » Today's date—and the date you intend to achieve your goal;
> » The person you are—strengths and abilities;
> » Your current situation relative to your dream—including employment, marital status, family status, health status, financial status, and personal growth status.

Be thorough, and be honest. Write it down in a journal, and keep it close at hand throughout your journey.

Setting A Strong Deadline

Our missions in the skies over Afghanistan were focused on providing support to ground forces. Those amazing warriors counted on us to be in the right place at the right time—every time.

There was no excuse for being behind schedule. On occasion, setbacks and challenges confronted us and put us behind; that's when tensions rose. We had a commitment to the mission to perform and deliver with precision.

Perhaps you have had a tight deadline or have operated in a similar situation where there was very little room for error. It could have been delivering a sales presentation, or delivering a baby. You may have had to raise money for a cause or raise a family.

In any case you have likely performed under tight deadlines.

One of the most significant drivers of success is the notion of a tight deadline. Regardless of how organized or driven you are, people have a tendency to push harder and focus more when a deadline is closer, as opposed to further away.

It is actually better to be under pressure than to have total time freedom. Sometimes the pressure of a deadline pushes us to perform at our best. The door to procrastination is open when we have seemingly unlimited time to accomplish our mission.

Take a look at the date you intend to accomplish your goal. What is it about that date that motivates you? Why are you striving to realize your vision by that date and time? Does that date push you to move toward it every day?

The notion that things tend to get done at the last minute holds true in lots of cases; when you squeeze yourself out of your comfort zone, interesting things happen that can work in your favor. This is not a "hall pass" for procrastinating until the last minute. Quite the opposite. This is simply a recognition of the power of focus, particularly when there is a lot on the line.

For one thing, your awareness of opportunities becomes more heightened. Because your goal is fast approaching, you start really focusing on the pertinent information and blocking out the nonessential noise. It's as if your brain senses an impending disaster and wants to protect itself from doom— you'll start seeing time, money, assets, and people show up in your life with your newfound focus.

Another benefit to pushing your target date and time forward is the sense of urgency that catapults your dream to a new level of priority. Your dream no longer takes a backseat to television and other distractions —it no longer permits the snooze button to be an option...

Perhaps one of the best attributes to having your highly-defined goal with a do-or-die, non-negotiable deadline is the boost in your sense of purpose. The whole world will receive you with more respect because you'll be carrying a different kind of posture: the posture of a person on purpose.

Tighten your timeline, narrow your focus, and apply the commitment you require to achieve your vision and your life will never be the same.

Changes To Your Flight Plan

Remember, even the best crafted flight plan can change. In aviation, the flight plan you file is rarely the one you fly—air traffic control, last minute adjustments to the mission, even changes in the lineup of your crew can alter the mission.

As a brand-new rookie pilot my crew was tasked to fly a reconnaissance mission on the one-year anniversary of 9/11. We were flying in the North Arabian Gulf, out of an airfield in the Middle East. Needless to say, tensions were high. All but two of us—our mission commander and me—had an intense stomach virus. Yet despite sickness and oppressive heat, the decision was made to press on and fly the mission.

Whether or not it was a sound decision is irrelevant. What I can tell you is this: as a crew, we were extremely hampered and limited in how well we could execute our mission that day. There were a lot of mentally and physically tough people operating well outside their normal capabilities, which is why the mission was accomplished.

To get it done, we altered our flight plan in a few critical ways. First, we adjusted the route of flight so as to arrive "on station"—the assigned area of our operations for that mission—ahead of schedule. This allowed the hampered crew members a few minutes to hydrate and possibly eat a snack to quell their uneasy stomachs.

In those extra few minutes, those of us who were not affected by the stomach virus hustled; we took care of other aspects of the mission called for later in the flight.

This made great use of our time and allowed us to focus on other aspects of the mission later on when we would have normally been addressing the things we took care of early.

We also took a quick inventory of our systems and found ways to maximize our fuel load. In a way, we "made fuel" simply by shutting down one of our 4 engines and conserving our limited supply in case we needed it to accomplish the mission.

The intent here is to illustrate how even in adversity, we found ways to create success—even in small parcels here and there.

The more flexible you are to change, the more creative you are in progressing toward your dream, the less the inevitable setbacks of high-achievement will steal your momentum.

In the words of the great Thomas Edison, "Everything comes to him who hustles while he waits."

Regardless of setbacks, the mission must get done. Sometimes you have to be flexible and prepared to alter course in order to see the mission through to the end.

Flying Your Flight Plan

Now that you have a specific and highly-defined goal, with a non-negotiable target date set, it's time to execute your flight plan. Imagine how amazing it will feel to arrive there. Celebrate it in your mind and get comfortable with the idea of success.

As you progressively work backward, note the importance of each step. Assign dates and times to these steps, and place them on a calendar so you can watch the visual progression as your track toward success.

And keep it simple—at least in the beginning. Don't concern yourself with every detail, or every step that will be required. Chances are you'll add steps later; perhaps you'll move steps in different order as the flight plan evolves. Strive to nail down five to ten critical steps in the beginning, then allow the process to illustrate the rest of the steps as you progress.

Final Checks

To this point, you've learned why now, more than ever, is the most critical time to go after your big dream, your ultimate vision.

You know that anything worth achieving will take time; but with a Flight Plan To Success™, you know when you'll achieve your dream, as well as the various checkpoint goals along the way.

You now know money is not a holdback to success, but a major power tool—necessary to attaining your goals. With the tools provided in this book, you can strategically and logically line up the money and streams of income necessary to achieve your dream.

You now know the assets and resources required to arrive at the destination of your dreams are all around you. In fact, *you have everything you need to accomplish anything you want.* You just have to look and ask for it.

You now know people are the cornerstones of your Flight Plan To Success™ —the key people you need are all around you. Sometimes they're obvious, and sometimes they'll surprise you. The key is to be open and be ready for them to arrive and deliver once you have sounded the call.

And, most importantly, you know you are the pilot of your dreams. Perhaps you've known it all along. You are an amazing performer when you act with confidence.

Go confidently, pursue passionately, and achieve spectacularly.

Climbing Into The Cockpit For Your Ultimate Mission

In aviation, we have a saying: Speed is Life. This is not meant as a brash or macho statement, but rather an axiom of flight.

You see the wing of aircraft works through pressure differentials. There's less air pressure on the top of the wing than there is on the bottom—the higher pressure below pushes, or lifts the wing. The more air passing across the surface of the wing, the greater the pressure differential, so speed equates to lift—speed is life.

Altitude is also an important element of flight. Flying low and fast over the ground makes for an exciting and exhilarating ride, but sooner or later, the mountains come up and you either have to climb or alter your course.

And flying an aircraft at higher altitudes comes with the added benefit of flying faster. The air at high altitude is less dense, and therefore creates less friction and makes higher speeds possible. Also, winds aloft—particularly from the massive river of high-speed winds called the Jet Stream—can act as a catapult to push an aircraft to fly faster.

Altitude in life is important as well. Altitude prevents small obstacles—even the bigger ones—from standing in the way of your dreams. And just as in an aircraft, the higher you fly, the further downrange you can see. Your vision literally expands when you adopt a High-Altitude mindset.

Speed and altitude in life come in the form of personal growth and knowledge. Some refer to that as wisdom; the combination of life's experiences with knowledge gained from books, lectures, articles, and more life experience.

Wisdom is a funny thing; it can create tyrants and it can create saviors. It can unlock the doors of terror, and it can answer the prayers of an entire world.

Whether you read this book again and again, share it with others to assist them to excel in life. You have the power to take your wisdom and change the world. You can create fortunes, provide solutions to challenges, and create a better life for yourself and your family.

The important point is to get up and do it. Don't delay. Don't wait for it to get easier, don't wait for the economy or the government to improve, don't wait for a point where you'll have more time because those days never come. There is no better time than right now, no better day than today, and no better person than you. You deserve it—the world deserves it—it's the reason you were put on the planet.

You have the knowledge and the tools—now you must choose to climb in the cockpit or stay on the ground.

Keeping The Mission In Perspective

As a kid growing up, my goal was to become a Blue Angel. But my passionate "why", or my vision, was to be the best I could be—to fly aircraft and inspire people.

My goal of becoming a Blue Angel never happened.

Shortly before I graduated flight school, my class and I handed in our "dream sheets"—basically, the types of aircraft we wanted to fly. I had always wanted to be a fighter pilot and fly jets; and that was a prerequisite for making the Blue Angels.

Aircraft selection is based on flight school grades and the needs of the Navy. Despite my high class ranking and strong flight school grades, the needs of the Navy didn't support enough jet slots for me to make it. Instead, I was assigned one of only two maritime patrol slots, which meant I was flying the P-3C Orion.

I was crushed.

Even though there were only two jet slots, and two P-3 slots, and the rest of the class was left with helicopters, I felt like the kid who got coal in his stocking on Christmas morning.

I knew of a handful of P-3 pilots who made the transition to the jet community after their first 4-years on a deployment cycle. But at that point, I was engaged to marry Mia and our daughter Callie was on the way. And since I was lucky to have received an awesome assignment flying logistics and sonobuoy test flights out of San Diego, I decided to put the jet dream to rest.

One day, as Mia and I crept along in traffic, an F/A-18 Hornet—the very aircraft flown by the Blue Angels, the one I had dreamt of flying—roared overhead.

I sighed and shook my head, "Shoulda, woulda, coulda."

"Excuse me?" Mia said.

"Nothing…just lamenting what could have been," I said.

"And now look how much greater your life has turned out. You're a husband. You're a father. You're a friend. And you're a leader. "

She finished that sentence with a nod of her head to the backseat of our car. One look over my shoulder and I could see the smiling face of my 2 year-old daughter, Callie; pigtails blowing in the breeze and animal cracker crumbs covering her "I love Daddy" t-shirt.

Mia was right. I was so wrapped up in achieving—in focusing on the destination—that I lost sight of my true vision. I was ungrateful for the blessings I had, the true miracle my life had become. Because I had associated myself with my goals—rather than my true vision—I was wallowing in self-pity.

I was living a life most people would kill for. I had an incredible career where I led bright people and made an impact on their lives. I got to fly airplanes almost every day—and had fun doing it. I was literally married to my dream girl—the most gorgeous woman I had ever met, my soul mate, the one who lit up my world (and continues to do so today). Had I flown anything other than the P-3, I might never had met Mia. I had an absolutely perfect daughter—bright, sweet, healthy, and happy who adored me (and still does). And soon, we would have a perfect son—bright, handsome, witty, and full of joy just to be in the same room with me.

All of this is the icing on the cake.

Through all I have accomplished, and all I have endured, some goals have been met, others have not. But what has remained alive, what has been fully realized, is my true life vision.

Remember to keep your goals in perspective. And back the currency of your goals with the gold standard of your vision. Because your goals do not define the person you are, but your true vision is as much a part of you as your soul.

Your goals are not the person you are; they are stepping stones to your ultimate dream, your true vision. Keeping the perspective of goals and dreams is critical to true happiness and fulfillment; knowing that your value is not determined by what you have accomplished but rather the person you had to become in order to accomplish it is the elixir of success. You are already successful, just for boldly going after your dream.

Flight School Is Over—It's Time To Fly

When I first started flight school, the only thing I could think of was my destination: earning my wings of gold and becoming a Naval Aviator. I thought about it, dreamt about it, and kept it in mind until September 7, 2001 when the dream became reality.

The days, weeks, and months following my graduation became mini-flight schools. We had the training and qualification to perform some of the most intense air operations in the world, and had accomplished something few people ever do. The percentage of people who aspire to become military aviators compared to the number who make it is so small.

I share this with you to put it all in perspective—you are now in a similar category. So many people want a better life and have big dreams, but so few ever do anything about it.

You will.

You've taken the first step toward success by investing your greatest asset—your time. You have your wings—now use them. Get out to the flight line of life and take off toward your dreams.

Again, be unreasonable in your dreams, but pragmatic in your approach.

You have a responsibility to dream the grandest dream you can, plan it intelligently, and pursue it passionately. You owe it to the world to be your best; the world needs more champions. You owe it to yourself to have everything in life you want. Now go out and get it.

Go for whatever fires you up and catapults you out of bed in the morning; set your sights on the loftiest dream you have. Keep your eyes on the prize and your feet on the ground with a logical, level-headed strategy for pursuing your dream.

Build your Flight Plan To Success™ and climb to higher altitudes than you ever have. As you climb, have faith: you'll likely encounter storms and turbulence along the way, but you're prepared. You will navigate all of it because you deserve your success and have planned to make it happen.

You will become the beacon of hope to the world around you, because they will see the transformation in you from dreamer to doer. You will fly to new heights and reach new levels of fulfillment you previously only dreamed of. With your Flight Plan To Success™ you will never see the world the same way. Now you will long to climb, long to soar, and long to achieve everything your vision calls you to do.

In the words of Leonardo da Vinci, "...and once you have tasted flight you will walk the earth with your eyes turned skyward, for there you have been and there you long to return."

And remember, no matter what course you fly in life,
Fly High, Fly Fast, Fly Far.
-JT

ABOUT THE AUTHOR

JT DeBolt is a success coach, inspirational keynote speaker, and former US Naval Aviator. He served over 12 years on active duty—working his way up from enlisted aircraft mechanic to combat-decorated Naval Aviator despite being turned down by the the US Navy six times. He served in Operations Desert Storm, Enduring Freedom, and Iraqi Freedom. JT completed his service in 2008 and began an entrepreneurial career with his wife, Mia, and is the CEO of DeBolt Enterprises, LLC.

While flying was a lifelong dream, JT found the most rewarding aspect of military service to be the leadership experience of serving with amazing men and women both as an enlisted sailor and naval officer. Today he carries that experience over into his coaching and consulting practice.

JT's coaching programs range from small groups to private one-on-one coaching, and includes the world's only mission accomplishment course, F.L.I.G.H.T. School To Success™.

As a dynamic inspirational speaker and Mission Accomplishment Expert, JT focuses on practical strategies to help organizations and individuals define and accomplish their missions in business and life.

JT leans on his leadership training and aviation background to lead and inspire fellow entrepreneurs to achieve their maximum potential in business and in life. Through the culmination of real-life lessons and practical military flight experience, JT empowers people to pursue and achieve their dreams, while creating a vision and a life by their design.

A graduate of University of Colorado at Boulder, JT is passionate about skiing and mountain biking, and loves hiking and camping with his wife, Mia, daughter, Callie, and son, Maximus. He is an ardent, lifelong fan and future owner of the NFL's Seattle Seahawks.